'Many books on bereavement offe[...] through grief and some helpful hin[...] testimony can be of equal, if not mc[...] so in the case of the loss of a child [...] [...]ct from the death of an adult, those who are bereft are not dealing with the discontinuation of the past, but the disappearance of an imagined future.

'This testimony by Karen Palmer is to be commended for its accuracy and its honesty, for recording hopes and disappointments, love and anger. And it is a testimony of faith. It admits to how the life God gives us is a life that is always at risk. Faith is not an insurance policy against disaster, but the means by which we can walk through the darkest of valleys and believe that there will yet be light.'
John L Bell, Iona Community

'This book is the record of the loss of a child, probably the most demanding experience this world can offer. The chapters are special because they are written by a doctor who understood the perils of an abnormal pregnancy, the wife of a minister of the gospel who shared the pain, and the daughter of another minister and his wife who had lost an infant son many years before. The book is also special because it is based on diaries kept at the time which bring out the authentic anguish and the surprising joy of the events before and after the birth and death of Jennifer Palmer. The grief is documented, but so are the indications of God's presence, love and care for Jennifer and her family.'
David Bebbington, Emeritus Professor of History, University of Stirling; former Deacon at Stirling Baptist Church

'To write about bereavement, especially a newborn, requires a very delicate touch. Those drawn to read are often either hurting themselves or know someone going through a similar trauma. Above all they want such writing to have a ring of truth to it that allows them to connect. I found myself drawn into the raw narrative, nodding my head in agreement. To make that link requires both honesty and vulnerability. Yet, alongside that, Karen brings her professional skills as a doctor and psychiatrist, and is able to helpfully self-reflect.

'In Jennifer's story there is no toning down the contrasting emotions, the contradictory thoughts or the imagined and feared scenarios. The faith that lifts the book is not a superhero faith but a learned experience of faith found through pain, not through an avoidance of reality. Supported by family, friends and her local congregation, Karen and Gordon are able to walk together through a year that changed their lives and the lives of those around them, and they invite us to join them on that journey.'
The Very Reverend Colin Sinclair, former Moderator of the General Assembly of the Church of Scotland

'I commend this beautiful book, which is both movingly sad and full of hope, because it will help those experiencing grief and especially any who have experienced the death of an infant. It certainly will do that, but in addition it is a testimony to the power of community in the face of human mortality and loss and to what it means for us to be the body of Christ in the world.'
Dr Stephen Chester, Lord and Lady Coggan Professor of New Testament, Wycliffe College, Toronto, Canada

'Jennifer Palmer's life by the world's measure would be seen as insignificant. She was born on 3rd August 1993, with an unknown fatal condition, and died the same day. However, God continues to use the testimony of her short and precious life and death. With soul-searching clarity, Karen Palmer, Jennifer's mother, writes her story here. She honestly shares her pain, anger, hopes and joy, while directing us to a loving God. Jennifer: A Life Precious to God is an invaluable book for anyone

who has experienced the death of a baby, or indeed is in a caring and supportive role to grieving parents.'
Judith Keefe, Founder of Under the Rainbow

'This is a beautiful book. It begins in heart-rending tragedy, but what unfolds is a testimony of hope and celebration. It's the story of how one young couple's hopes for a perfect baby were brutally crushed, and how, in the agony of their heartbreak, God spoke to them of the preciousness and importance of this tiny, damaged life growing within. It's about their faithfulness to that voice and its invitation to love and protect and nurture the fragile life they co-created, and the transforming and healing power of that love – in their own lives and those of many beyond.

'This is not a heroic story – although there is great courage and grit here. Rather it's a witness to the way that communities – church, friends and acquaintances – and the kindness of strangers can sustain us when we are at our most vulnerable and dependent. It's a story that goes right to the heart of the Christian faith and reminds us that God so often uses what we might reject or discount to embody and reveal His unconditional love and gentleness.

'Karen Palmer writes beautifully, and with honesty, humility and humour. I found this a hard book to put down: it's a gripping read, and, like Jennifer's brief life, its resonances will travel far and wide and deep.'
Dr Margaret Masson, Principal of St Chad's College, Durham

'In 1993, Rachel and I lived about a hundred yards from Karen and Gordon in Ruchazie. They were cherished friends and mentors during the almost six years we lived in that troubled and treasured place. We wept and walked and worshipped with them through the months described in this book. When, years later, we welcomed a pregnancy ourselves, with accompanying fears and decisions about tests, Jennifer's story was very present

for me. In some ways this is a polished gem of a book, honed by years of reflection, and in other respects it reads as raw as the grief it records. Although it touches on crucial medical–ethical issues, it is not an argument but a testimony – a testimony of faith, hope and love. It, like the woman who has written it, is brimming with tenderness and honesty and faith. I am so glad to have read it, and I recommend it to you unreservedly.'
Rev Dr Doug Gay, Lecturer in Practical Theology, University of Glasgow; Kirk Minister

'This deeply moving testimony about the short life of Karen Palmer's baby daughter Jennifer will bring great comfort to all who suffer the loss of a baby either during pregnancy or shortly after birth. The author brings the insight of a doctor, the passion of a grieving mother and the convictions of a strong Christian to this profoundly honest and transparent account of a journey of joy and sadness, fear and faith, despair and hope. We see Jennifer through her mother's eyes as a real person and family member, treasured, loved and enjoyed, and her loss as a temporary, painful separation before an eternity of future communion. Essential reading for pastors, doctors and others who journey with those facing early bereavement.'
Peter Saunders, CEO of International Christian Medical and Dental Association (ICMDA)

[Handwritten inscription:] to Gordon + Sarah Remembering too, your precious daughter Jennifer. with many thanks for your kind letter referenced on P132 Karen S Palmer

Jennifer

A Life Precious to God

The story behind 'A Cradling Song'

Karen S Palmer

instant apostle

First published in Great Britain in 2020

Instant Apostle
The Barn
1 Watford House Lane
Watford
Herts
WD17 1BJ

Copyright © Karen Palmer 2020

The author has asserted her rights under Section 77 of the Copyright, Designs and Patents Act, 1988, to be identified as the author of the work.

All rights reserved. No portion of this book may be reproduced or transmitted in any form or by any means, electronic or mechanical, including photocopying and recording, or by any information storage and retrieval system, without permission in writing from the publisher.

Cover image: copyright © Robin Love. Baby boots courtesy of Kimberley from Heidihousecrafts.

Unless otherwise indicated, all Scripture quotations are taken from the Good News Bible © 1994 published by the Bible Societies/HarperCollins Publishers Ltd UK, Good News Bible© American Bible Society 1966, 1971, 1976, 1992. Used with permission.

Scripture quotations marked 'NIV' are taken from the Holy Bible, New International Version® Anglicised, NIV® Copyright © 1979, 1984, 2011 by Biblica, Inc.® Used by permission. All rights reserved worldwide.

Extract from the song 'Rejoice, Rejoice' by Graham Kendrick copyright © Thankyou Music. Adm by Capitol CMG Publishing worldwide exc. UK & Europe, admin by Integrity Music, part of the David C Cook family, songs@integritymusic.com

Material indicated thus * is copyright WGRG The Iona Community and is published here with full permission.

Thanks to John Bell for permission to publish the words of 'A Cradling Song'.

Thanks to Gordon and Sarah Brown for permission to cite an extract of their letter.

Every effort has been made to seek permission to use copyright material reproduced in this book. The publisher apologises for those cases where permission might not have been sought and, if notified, will formally seek permission at the earliest opportunity.

The views and opinions expressed in this work are those of the author and do not necessarily reflect the views and opinions of the publisher.

British Library Cataloguing-in-Publication Data

A catalogue record for this book is available from the British Library.

This book and all other Instant Apostle books are available from Instant Apostle:

Website: www.instantapostle.com

Email: info@instantapostle.com

ISBN 978-1-912726-27-1

Printed in Great Britain.

Some names have been changed.

For Ruth and Sally

everywhere she had been there
grew flowers

A144 864   930359

DELIVERY

LLSCS   Born 09.52) 3 /
                Adm. 10:15) / 8 /
                                    / 93

Jennifer grace
Baby PALMER

Sex   Relig.   Weight

F   2.22 kg

Jennifer's cot card

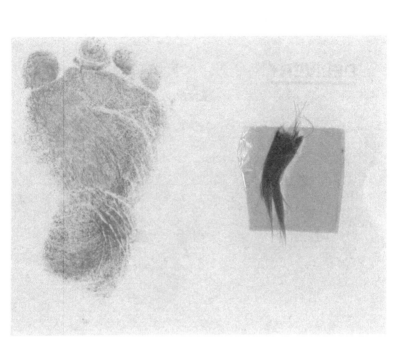

Jennifer's footprint and a lock of hair

Contents

Foreword 17

Preface, by Gordon R Palmer 20

Christmas 25

Easter 29

Continuing 47

Preparing 50

Help 55

Hope 59

Arrival – 'A Day of Unexpected Grace' 65

Home 85

Letting Go 88

Gifts 105

Flowers in the Wilderness 109

Grace Abounding 114

A Promise Fulfilled 133

Glory to God 134

Acknowledgements 142

Useful Links and Resources 146

Bibliography 150

Foreword

I once stumbled upon a television talk show where the host was whipping up the audience to argue among themselves about which was the most painful loss – that of a spouse, a parent or a child. It seemed callous and pointless. The fact is, none of us can truly compare our grief journey with anyone else's. Nicholas Wolterstorff, writer and theologian, has used the word 'inscape'[1] to describe the internal landscape of each bereavement – different for each person grieving and for each person lost to them. Billions of permutations and combinations of experiences and emotions are possible, making every loss, every tale of grief, unique.

This book is one story of one loss (our first daughter, Jennifer) set in one place: central Scotland. It begins in a small but character-filled housing scheme, Ruchazie, by far the friendliest place I have ever lived, where Gordon and I embarked on married life.

Despite those particulars, I hope this book will help others who find themselves in the position we did of knowing that something is very wrong during pregnancy, or who have lost a child in other circumstances. I hope

---

[1] Nicholas Wolterstorff, *Lament for a Son* (Grand Rapids, MI: William B Eerdmans Publishing Co, 1987).

that, as you read, you'll see me wrestling with thoughts you have experienced, and feel less alone. Along the way, you will discover what helped us and what didn't, and through those sections, hopefully relatives, friends, pastors, church leaders, medical and allied professionals will pick up hints on how better to care. Please have a look at the bibliography and useful links section at the end of the book; hopefully you will find something there that will also be a help and support. Wonderfully, there are now resources available at the click of a button, which wasn't the case when we were expecting Jennifer – for her story is also set in one particular time.

Jennifer would have been twenty-seven years old this year (2020), so why only write about her now? Because it's an amazing story – not about me, but about Jennifer herself and how God stepped in and carried us, as we carried her. Retirement from work brought time to write, and also a sense of urgency, a desire to make sure that her story is passed down through the generations of our family – especially when we have a hymn in the fourth edition of the Church of Scotland's *Church Hymnary* (CH4) written for us and its tune named for her;[2] a desire, too, to be able to tell her story to a wider audience, because it's undoubtedly good news. It's about God loving us, even

---

[2] *Church Hymnary Fourth Edition*, music edition (Norwich: Canterbury Press, 2005). Hymn 733. Tune: *Jennifer*. Words and Music: John Bell. This hymn originally appeared as 'A Cradling Song' in John L Bell and Graham Maule, *When Grief is Raw: Songs for Times of Sorrow and Bereavement* (Glasgow: Wild Goose Resource Group, Wild Goose Publications, the Iona Community, 1997).

when we can't do that ourselves, and about Him coming right up close and involving Himself with us.

Through the story of Jennifer, you will hear of a God who loves us more than we can possibly imagine. He loves us in all our mess, all our failures, all our weakness. My prayer is that, if you don't already know Him, you'll find Him in these pages and your eyes will be opened to His love for you. Perhaps you do know Him, but you've not yet learned that you can completely trust Him. Hopefully, as you read, you'll see what a difference it can make to depend on His promises, which He always keeps.

This book is about the treasure of every life and the treasure of knowing a God who is with us. Thank you for reading it. May God bless you and speak to you as you do.
Karen S Palmer

Preface
By Gordon R Palmer

'Do you have children? How many?'

It's an innocent enough question which comes up not infrequently. After many years, I still don't know how best to answer it. I usually say, 'Two.' To explain that I have three children, but one died hours after her birth, means upsetting the enquirer, making them feel awkward, and leaving me feeling awkward too. It's much easier to say, 'Two' – even though I feel disloyal towards Jennifer when I do, and also that a part of me is being denied. It's always been so. I'm Jennifer's dad.

In the book, Karen mentions being at a wedding soon after we had had Jennifer. After the groom's father had expressed his condolences, I recall saying to him that Karen and I were glad we were able to be there. Were we? Of course we were – at one level. But at another we knew, we all knew, that we were only able to be there because Jennifer was no longer with us. A double-edged sword.

This book has taken shape around diaries that Karen kept at the time, including one she began to write during the pregnancy for Jennifer. She has kept similar for our other daughters. It is therefore immediate, expressing first thoughts and reactions. It is reflective, as Karen in particular thought deeply about all that was going on. It is also honest, as diaries should be and often are. Some other bits and pieces from the time also feature: some words of family and friends; a tribute that Karen and I put together for the funeral which was read by our friend Alistair Drummond; and, of course, 'A Cradling Song' – a hymn now in CH4 and written by John L Bell. A couple of years ago, I was surprised and delighted as I sat in a friend's house and her sister, who had not known about the origins of the hymn, reeled off the first verse – more word perfectly that I could have, or can.

It is because experiences like this can strike so many chords with other people that this story is told. It does help us to know that out of the worst thing that has ever happened to us, some lasting good has come. That does not justify what happened to Jennifer. Again, a double-edged sword.

The story is also told because we feel deeply thankful to so many people who were such a help to us. And it is told because our awareness of and love for God was deepened – even though we could never tell why this should have happened to us. Would it have helped to know? I doubt it. There are some things that can never be explained or justified. 'For now we see only a reflection as in a mirror; then we shall see face to face. Now I know in part; then I shall know fully, even as I am fully known' (1 Corinthians 13:12, NIV).

The day that I began to think that you might exist was one of the most beautiful I have ever seen. It was the Monday before Christmas. There was a covering of snow everywhere – on the trees and fields, and the sky was a pale pink. It looked so perfect and so peaceful that my heart felt like bursting in praise to God. I was listening to a tape by Ian White called 'Psalms'[3] and the words seemed to sum up how I was feeling, and confirm God's love and care, no matter what the future was to hold.

Jennifer's Diary, December 1992

[3] Ian White, *Psalms Volume One*, Little Misty Music, 1985.

Jennifer Grace:

It was Christmas Eve when we heard that you were coming. We made jokes about seeing wise men wandering about Ruchazie following a star! But Christmas did seem such a good time to hear about you, our gift from God; and it made Christmas extra special for your grandparents, aunts and uncles.

We enjoyed sharing such happy news with family and friends. Soon a hospital scan showed you, with arms and legs waving, no bigger than a butter bean; that was your first name – 'Butter bean'. Later, we heard your heartbeat – it was a wooshing kind of sound; that was your second name – 'Woosh-woosh'. Then we could feel, and even see, your first kicks.

Gordon's tribute, August 1993

Christmas

I'd been wanting to be pregnant for so long, that when it happened, it seemed too good to be true. Gordon and I had married in 1987, the day before my graduation in Medicine, and we had agreed to delay having a family until my specialty training was complete. It was a crazy beginning to married life – having not been certain that Gordon was definitely going to propose, I had arranged my Resident posts at the Inverclyde Royal Hospital in Greenock, where I would get valuable experience, even though Gordon had applied to be minister of Ruchazie Church of Scotland in the East End of Glasgow. Thirty miles of busy M8 motorway separated the two, and in 1987, before European working time directives and pressure from the Royal Colleges, junior doctors worked a ridiculous number of hours each week. It was possible, during a weekend, to be working continuously, without any sleep, for forty hours!

At least, because we were married and therefore living together, when I did have a night or a weekend off, I was able to go home and see him, rather than use one of the rooms assigned for Residents at the hospital.

For our second year of married life, I applied for a post in psychiatry at Duke Street Hospital in Glasgow (much nearer home) and then joined the psychiatry training scheme for the East End of Glasgow. Membership exams for the Royal College of Psychiatrists were in two parts – and I eventually passed Part Two in May 1992.

Had we started trying for a family before then? Certainly, at some stage we had gone to our General Practitioner (GP), concerned that it was taking a long time for me to conceive, and around the time of that pale pink sky in December our appointment card for the fertility clinic had dropped through our letter box. Instead, we attended the antenatal clinic where, at ten weeks, on 28th January, an ultrasound scan showed a tiny form with arms and legs that waved. I declined a blood test for detecting spina bifida and related conditions, and that first decision seemed easy.

My training rotation had placed me in the Royal Scottish National Hospital (RSNH) in Larbert. A hospital for patients with severe learning disabilities, many of whom had been there for decades, it was not a place conducive to taking the birth of a healthy baby for granted. While Gordon relished telling his parishioners our good news, I was much more hesitant. I knew most miscarriages happened before twelve weeks, however, and so reaching that stage in February seemed reason for rejoicing. Catherine, a lovely music therapist whose office was just along the corridor from mine was at the same stage of pregnancy, so we decided to hit the shops and buy something for our babies in celebration.

I began to feel much more confident about the pregnancy, but it bothered me that I didn't have much of a bump. In March, at a routine antenatal appointment, my midwife was also concerned, but the height of my uterus was fine, and when her probe found the sound of the baby's heart, we both heaved sighs of relief.

On the morning of Sunday 4th April, Dad felt you kick for the first time. It was as if you knew, because, before he felt with his hand, your movements were quite gentle. After a few seconds of your dad's hand being there, you gave a kick that he couldn't miss! You were nineteen weeks and four days old. The next day we found out that you were very sick.

Jennifer's Diary, April 1993

Easter

By now I was on a forensic psychiatry placement at the State Hospital, Carstairs. On the Monday of Holy Week, however, a heavy cold had kept me awake most of the night and I stayed at home. Anxious that I hadn't felt the baby move for several hours, I stood naked in front of a mirror and reckoned that I didn't look pregnant at all. Increasingly alarmed, I phoned my midwife at Rottenrow Hospital[4] and she arranged to meet us there. Again, she examined me, and hearing the now familiar wooshing of our baby's heartbeat, Gordon and I could have happily returned home there and then, completely reassured. I didn't understand our midwife's enthusiasm for another ultrasound scan.

It took three times up on the table, with frantic drinking of water in between, before the radiographer was satisfied with the size of my bladder. She began moving the probe over my gelled-up abdomen, looking at the pale shapes on the screen, and from where I lay, I could see her panic increasing. She started taking photographs, and issued an

---

[4] Glasgow Royal Maternity Hospital was known through all of Glasgow as Rottenrow, the name of an adjacent, steeply inclining street, itself known locally as Induction Hill.

urgent request for a doctor. When none came, she left in search of one.

And so, a young, ponytailed, male doctor entered the room, silently picked up the probe and began to explore the images of our baby himself. After a minute or so, he apologised for his silence and introduced himself as Dr Matthew. He asked if my 'waters had broken', which they had not, and then asked if anything ran in our families in the way of disorders, immediately apologising, saying I must have been asked that already. Then, still scanning, he asked if I was working, and what I worked as. His relief that I was a doctor was visible, and he said something about how it would make everything easier to explain. He asked Gordon if he was working, and Dr Matthew told us that his father was also a Church of Scotland minister.

He then took us through what he had found – lack of fluid around the baby, tiny kidneys, squarish ribs, a cyst at one end of the spine, an enlarged space in the lining of the brain, and an arm that looked like a claw, with a drooped and apparently useless hand. Our baby immediately became a hideous 'thing' to me – ugly and misshapen. It didn't even cross our minds to ask its sex. He took measurements, photographs, even a video. All I could think about was my bladder.

Scan over, I was eventually able to escape to the toilets and concentrated hard on keeping my mind blank until I was back at Gordon's side. We were led to an attractive cubicle where we sat with Dr Matthew while he struggled to tell us what he believed he had seen and its significance. When he had first come into the scanning room, I assumed that the radiographer had just grabbed the first doctor she could find, but we were beginning to recognise his expertise.

He meant to tell us that the machine he had just used was the top ultrasound machine, but said instead that we had had the top ultrasonographer, but then laughed and said some would say that was also true. He was funny, yet warm and obviously concerned about us. He said the baby was abnormal, but he had no idea what was wrong – all the abnormalities were very subtle but because there were so many, they added up to something big. He was unable to give us an accurate prognosis, but felt it was likely that the pregnancy would not go to term. He told us all the hospital could offer was a diagnosis, but that that was important, for the sake of future children.

Testing for chromosome disorders using amniocentesis (sampling of the fluid) would be impossible, as there was so little fluid around our baby. Using chorionic villus sampling (CVS) to obtain cells from the placenta for testing was still an option. Dr Matthew did not want us to make any decisions there and then, but suggested we go home, let the news settle, and return three days later, on the Thursday.

I remember feeling dazed, and him leaning forward, gently saying, 'What I am telling you is very bad news,' as if afraid we had not understood.

CVS sounded very reasonable to me that morning.

We left the hospital and went by car to do a few chores. Arriving home, we realised we were very hungry, and prepared lunch. Gordon started to give thanks to God for the food, and broke down in terrible sobs. Married for nearly six years, I had never seen him cry before. I clung to him and it felt then as if we were drowning and wouldn't cope. We cried for our hoped-for normal baby whom we had lost. Our distress frightened me. All our previously held principles faded with the initial horror of this 'thing' inside me. My stomach hurt, and I remember thinking, 'Oh good – I'm going to lose it now.' I felt as if I was no longer pregnant. I wondered whom we could call to come and help us. It didn't seem like the kind of news to give to close family over the telephone.

That afternoon, Gordon was due to pick up a new-to-us car, so, on the pretence of showing it to his parents, we drove it the short distance to their house in East Kilbride. Sitting in their living room, Gordon was quiet and I did the talking, explaining that the baby was 'abnormal'. Betty came and put her arms round me, and Robert, grief-stricken, just said, 'Why? Why?' over and over again. Betty went to put the kettle on and Robert asked whether, if we were going to have an abortion, it would be on Thursday when we were due to return to the hospital. I said we hadn't discussed anything yet. A termination of pregnancy (TOP) was never a possibility with me, but it felt like the pregnancy was already over. Betty offered me coffee, and although I had been completely off the taste for months, I drank it.

That evening, in Ruchazie church building, we had the first of our Holy Week services.

Ruchazie, designated by the Church of Scotland as an 'Urban Priority Area' and by Glasgow District Council as an 'Area of Deprivation', had enormous unemployment, and social problems were rife. Gordon had found that

We heard that you were sick. It was the
Monday of Easter week.
Gordon's tribute, August 1993

John L Bell, the hymn writer, had a special gift for tuning into the hardship and despair experienced by so many in our community, and so the words of his songs and readings had authenticity and relevance. We often used the responsive readings from *A Wee Worship Book*,*[5] because they helped the whole congregation feel more involved in the service. Our church was small but very committed and several of us often worked together to plan services. That was particularly the case for Holy Week when we had a service every evening, and so Gordon had shared out the preparation among a number of us.

On the Sunday afternoon, eight days before the life-changing ultrasound scan, I had still been in innocent bliss. I had met up with Jo, one of our Careforce[6] workers, to plan our allotted service, which happened to be for that first Monday of Holy Week. Gordon had chosen the week's theme – 'Good News' – and the title he had given us was 'Good News for the Unimportant'.

That Sunday afternoon, Jo and I prepared the whole thing, choosing songs and responses, mostly taken straight from *A Wee Worship Book* or slightly adapted. Unknown to us, on that Sunday, God was preparing all that Gordon and I and the rest of our small church would need to hear a week and a day later.

---

[5] Material throughout the book which is indicated thus * is copyright Wild Goose Resource Group (WGRG), the Iona Community and is published here with full and kind permission.
[6] Careforce was a Christian charity that matched young people on gap years with small inner-city churches. Founded in 1980, it sadly had to close in 2012 owing to lack of funds.

HOLY WEEK SERVICE
MONDAY 5th APRIL 1993
"GOOD NEWS FOR ..... THE UNIMPORTANT"

OPENING RESPONSES

Leader- O God, who created the heavens and stretched them out
ALL   - WE PRAISE YOU!
L   - You fashioned the earth and all that lives there
ALL   - WE PRAISE YOU!
L   - You give breath to the people upon it
        And spirit to those who walk on it
ALL   - WE PRAISE AND THANK YOU, O GOD!
L   - That the eyes of the blind be opened,
        The broken hearts be healed,
        The poor hear the good news,
        The captives be brought out of darkness
ALL   - YOUR KINGDOM COME, O LORD.
        YOUR WILL BE DONE.
L   - So shall we sing a new song, O Lord
ALL   - AND PRAISE YOUR NAME FOREVER

* God say -
"How can I give you up?
How can I abandon you?
My heart will not let me do it
My love for you is too strong...
For I am God, and not man.
I, the Holy One, am with you"

SONG - LC 117 "Make Way"
"HOW CAN I GIVE YOU UP?"*
Reading - Mark 10 w 46 >52 page 61
"HOW CAN I GIVE YOU UP?"*
Reading - Luke 14 w 16 > 24 page 98

SONG - LC 166 "The Day of the Lord shall come."

PRAYER -   PTO for words.

Leader - Let us pray.
         Lord God,
         In Jesus, you touched the scabby
                    listened to the ignored
                    gave the depressed something to hope for
ALL   - Thankyou, Lord God, that all of us are
         important to you
L   - You bandaged the broken with love, and you healed them
ALL   - Thankyou, Lord God, that all of us are
         important to you
L   - We believe that your power to heal is still present,
         so on your help we call,
         Remembering those whose minds are menaced by thoughts
                          which worry or wound them
                    those whose hearts are broken because love has gone
                          or because the light they lived by
                          has turned to darkness

                                    PTO

Leader (contd) -

those whose feet walk in circles
stopping only when they are tired,
resting only to walk in circles again,
those whose flesh and bone or mind and spirit
are filled with pain,
those who feel discarded or disposable

ALL — O Christ, put your hands where our prayers beckon,
and thankyou that all of us are important to you.

SONG - LC 163 "Take this moment" (See below)

CLOSING RESPONSES:

Leader — The desert will sing and rejoice
ALL — AND THE WILDERNESS BLOSSOM WITH FLOWERS
L. — All will see the Lord's splendour
ALL — SEE THE LORD'S GREATNESS AND POWER

L — Tell everyone who is anxious
ALL — BE STRONG AND DON'T BE AFRAID
L — The blind will be able to see
ALL — THE DEAF WILL BE ABLE TO HEAR
L — The lame will leap and dance
ALL — THOSE WHO CAN'T SPEAK WILL SHOUT
L — This is the promise of the Lord
ALL — HIS PROMISE WILL BE FULFILLED.

Amen.

The Day of the Lord shall come.
(last verse + chorus:-
The Day of the Lord shall come
but now is the time
to subvert earth's wisdom
with Christ's folly sublime;
by loving the loveless,
turning the tide + the cheek
by walking beneath the cross
in step with the weak
— The desert shall spring to life,
the hills shall rejoice,
the lame of the earth shall leap,
the dumb shall find voice,
the lamb with the lion shall lie,
and the last shall be first,
and the nations for war no more
shall study or thirst

Take this Moment
(1st + 4th verses):-

Take this moment, sign + space,
take my friends around,
here among us make the place
where Your love is found.

Take the little child in me,
scared of growing old;
help him/her here to find his/her worth
made in Christ's own mould.

Of course, the original plan had been that Jo and I would lead the service together, but our other Careforce worker, another Karen, kindly took my place. Gordon had already given our deaconess, Janet Anderson, our news and by the time the service began, everyone in the small gathering was aware of our situation.

On the day that the question of termination had not been mentioned but had been implied, and on the day I felt relieved that I might miscarry, God used words put together by Jo and myself eight days previously, when we had had no knowledge of my baby's problems – words that the Wild Goose Resource Group (WGRG) had adapted from Hosea chapter 11:

> How can I give you up?
> How can I abandon you?
> My heart will not let me do it.
> My love for you is too strong,
> For I am God and not man.
> I, the Holy One, am with you.*

In the course of the service we had planned, those words were to be read out not once, but twice! There was also a response which everyone, together, had to say out loud, not just twice, but three times: 'Thank you, Lord God, that all of us are important to you.'

We were all awestruck; it was as if God was speaking directly to our baby. No one could have written a service that spoke more clearly of the value of our baby to Him, no matter how 'abnormal'! He loved her so much, He said that there was no way He, God (Almighty God!), was going to give her up or abandon her. By making the whole congregation affirm three times, 'all of us are important to you', it was as if God was driving the message of her worth home to us, so that in our dazed and stupefied state, we couldn't mistake it. John Bell's words in the closing song, 'Take this Moment', were used by God and given an additional, startling layer of meaning:

> Take this little child in me,
> Scared of growing old;
> Help her here to find her worth
> Made in Christ's own mould.*

As we spoke together the closing responses, God impressed on us the hope there is for His people. We were to be strong and neither to fear nor be anxious, we declared together, for no matter how damaged any of us was, one day we would all be whole, and that was God's certain promise. The whole congregation was amazed. That service left us in no doubt that God knew exactly what was going on, and that our child was precious to Him. God said He wouldn't abandon her, so how could we?

The scan results were clearly still playing havoc with my ability for rational thought, however, as the next morning found me trying to get into favourite needle-cord jeans which I hadn't been able to wear for weeks. I had telephoned the medical secretary at the State Hospital to let her know there was a problem with the pregnancy and that I would be absent for a few days. Gordon and I were therefore free to go to Stirling to see my parents. I wept in my father's arms as Gordon broke the news, and again we described our baby as 'abnormal'.

How I grew to hate that word! Love for this new unexpected, imperfect baby was beginning to bud, and with it, resentment grew at such cold, detached and unloving vocabulary. To say it was 'sick' resulted in assumptions from others that there must be some treatment, and there was none. We needed people to understand, but using the words that would best make them understand seemed harsh and horrible.

I remember describing to my mother that we were moving through two phases: having to grieve for the normal baby we had dreamt of, and then having to love and accept this other baby. I was wrong about there being only two phases, but that was enough to cope with then.

Back home in Ruchazie, we received a call from Dr John Baird, my consultant at the State Hospital. A kind, gracious man, typically he had tried to be in touch with us as soon as his secretary had passed on our news. I gave him the details of the scan results and relayed to him what Dr Matthew had said.

Tuesday evening brought with it the second of our Holy Week services, this time prepared by Betsy Chester, a primary school teacher and one of our elders who, again, had had no knowledge of Jennifer's problems as she had sat down to plan it several days before. The theme Gordon had given her was 'Good News for the Broken'. She chose another of John Bell's songs, 'We Cannot Measure How You Heal', and so, as the service drew to an end, we all as a congregation sang the words:

> We cannot measure how you heal
> Or answer every sufferer's prayer,

Yet we believe your grace responds
Where faith and doubt unite to care.
Your hands, though bloodied on the cross
Survive to hold and heal and warn,
To carry all through death to life
And cradle children yet unborn.*

And so, over the next few days, with the Holy Week services speaking so clearly and directly of God's love for this child, the piece of driftwood that we found and clung to was that even this tiny, damaged life was precious and should not be abandoned. As if conscious of the need to remind us of its importance, the baby kicked more energetically during these days than it had ever done before.

We had been contacting everyone we knew to tell them about our crisis. This was in the days before mobile phones, so texting was not an option, and, of course, there was no social media. After one or two awkward phone calls to friends, we realised what a difficult position we were putting them in, so began writing letters instead. In some, I wrote, 'Please phone,' and people did. We wanted people to know because we wanted them all to pray and we desperately needed their friendship and support. It was like throwing out a huge safety net. I wrote letter after letter – using 'snail mail' it would be a week or so before replies began to come, but with each one came more strength. The fewer people we had to tell ourselves, the better for us and the recipient, so we were especially grateful for people who offered or agreed to tell other friends or colleagues – we didn't want it kept quiet. The more people who knew, the less chance there would be of

Every evening of that week, we were reminded again and again of how much God loves you and how precious you are to Him. We even sang a song about Jesus cradling children yet unborn, so we knew that He was gently caring for you, even while you were sick.

Jennifer's Diary, April 1993

someone 'putting their foot in it' and their agony adding to ours.

Gordon phoned his parents to see how they were coping, and my brothers phoned me, one admitting that he had hoped for the answering machine so that he could have left his message of love and sympathy and then escaped!

With Thursday approaching, it became urgently important that we work out whether or not we should have CVS. Dr Matthew had said that a diagnosis was important for the sake of our future children, but had also explained that CVS carried a slight risk of miscarriage. As Christians, then, should Gordon and I prioritise as yet non-existent children rather than our living baby? I wasn't at all certain that I was thinking straight, but Gordon looked to me, as a doctor, to know what to do. It was in the days before the internet, but I pulled all my *Ethics & Medicine* journals and Christian Medical Fellowship magazines down from the shelves, and pored through my books on Christian ethics; there was nothing about prenatal testing of any kind, never mind CVS.

By Wednesday night, I was growing towards the certainty that we shouldn't have CVS or any other procedure which might carry any risk to our baby. If CVS could be of no benefit to this particular baby, and might even harm it, then surely we shouldn't have it. The thought of those imaginary 'future children' whom Dr Matthew had mentioned was so alluring, but our present baby was real and precious, and we should put its needs first. But I was grieving, and still feeling muddled and confused; and I knew that bereavement is never a good time to make major decisions. I phoned another doctor friend who hadn't yet heard of our situation and urged him to listen to our arguments against CVS to see if they made sense. What a terrible thing to spring on him, and then expect a cohesive reply! I was so grateful for the matter-of-fact way he coped with my questions, and he reassured me that my thoughts were still rational and my arguments sound. It seems a straightforward decision now, but I was haunted with how reasonable I had thought CVS had sounded on the Monday, and was worried that Dr Matthew would make it sound reasonable again.

On the Thursday morning, Gordon and I felt like we were going to sit an exam. We told ourselves that we couldn't be told anything worse than we had heard already. We wrote our list of questions at breakfast, having not been capable of writing them together beforehand.

At the hospital, we were put in the same pleasant cubicle and offered tea or coffee; we were able to joke about the gravity of a situation that calls for cups of tea.

Dr Matthew went through all of our questions and we were touched by how difficult he was finding it. CVS, he confirmed, would be of no benefit to this baby. He said it was clear we wanted to continue with the pregnancy no matter what, and if that was the case, then it would in fact be inconsistent to have CVS. Having been scared of being talked round, it was a huge relief to have our decision accepted. Dr Matthew offered to arrange a second opinion, but over the week we had heard of his good reputation in this field, and declined. Again, he said that he had a hunch the pregnancy wouldn't go to term, but he also couldn't guarantee that I wouldn't give birth to a live baby who would need a lot of looking after for many years. He was kind and supportive and agreed to keep a careful eye on me for the next few months.

When we left that appointment, we asked each other if we were OK, in the same way that you count your fingers after someone has given you a very vigorous handshake. We were, partly because we had heard nothing worse than on the Monday, and we were well on the way to adjusting to the news we had heard then. That adjustment had been much aided by all the talking and writing we had done since. There's also no doubt that we were being sustained by a huge mobilised praying army – and by the knowledge given to us from the Holy Week services of God's presence and care.

> ... Easter week, we were thinking about God's suffering with us and so we knew that Jesus understood our pain.
> Gordon's tribute, August 1993

All that had happened, and the clarity of God speaking to us among it all, was affecting more than just Gordon and me. A letter from my parents arrived in which they wrote, 'Even already, God has used this experience in your life to help us.'

The Saturday of Holy Week comes between the day Christians remember Jesus' death and the day we celebrate His resurrection. It's a time of waiting: a time of silence from heaven, such that hopelessness and despair can have free reign.

On the Saturday of Holy Week, the lively and energetic kicks of our baby stopped and, for an anxious while, my womb was still. I saw that we had worked hard to get over the loss of our imagined perfect child, and had begun to love this other child, but not quite registered that there would be a third phase – that of grieving for our baby whenever it died. That was frightening, and confusing. It was hard to be only beginning to love someone whom we knew we were very likely to lose.

With Easter Sunday and the rest of the Easter season came more promises, however, and more encouragement.

Sunday brought the promise of resurrection and so we knew that whatever happened, it would not be the end.
Gordon's tribute, August 1993

EVENING SERVICE   18/4/93

Leader: God is our shelter and strength, always ready
         to help in times of trouble.
All   : The Lord Almighty is with us!
Leader: When we are afraid he comforts us.
All   : The Lord Almighty is with us!
Leader: When we are sad he brings us joy.
All   : The Lord Almighty is with us!
Leader: God is always with us and he cannot be
         defeated.
All   : The Lord Almighty is with us!
Leader: He rules over all the world and brings peace
         where there is strife.
All   : The Lord Almighty is with us!
Leader: Who is with us?
All   : The Lord Almighty is with us!
Leader: Will he ever leave us?
All   : No!
Leader: The Lord Almighty is with us! He reigns
         supreme for ever!
All   : Hallelujah!

Continuing

When I returned to work after the public holidays of Easter weekend, apart from the briefest of greetings, I was met with complete silence by the doctors I shared an office with. No eye contact, no questions, no concern. Going into the medical secretaries' room in order to fetch some case notes elicited the same response – baffling! They were all lovely people – it was bewildering and made no sense. I approached our own secretary and asked if Dr Baird had told her about the scan. Indeed he had, but she and the other secretaries, as well as my roommates, had taken it for granted that I wouldn't continue with the pregnancy. They assumed I had had an abortion. Once I explained the misunderstanding, they could not have been kinder or more concerned for me.

I had been given a disturbing insight into what the experience of someone who had been in the same situation as us, but had opted for a TOP, might entail – someone who also had planned for and looked forward to their child, whose dreams had also been cut short, who was truly bereaved: someone who, therefore, even more so, needed care and compassion. That seemed strange to me, when society was so apparently accepting of the thousands of TOPs which took place in our country every week.

The months that followed were hard. We had tremendous support from all of my colleagues, from family, friends, church – even people we had never met – and we needed every ounce of it.

[We] thank God that where we cannot trace meaning we can still be assured that our heavenly Father understands and His presence and His promises remain unshakeable realities. Please assure Gordon and Karen that Isobel and I, like many others, will have them in our hearts and in our prayers.
Peter Barber, in a letter to my parents

Very sorry to hear your difficult news. It sounds unspeakably painful but an experience you are already finding the Lord use to show His ideas in. We bow before His majesty and love, and feel for you in your confusion of emotions.
Susan and Patrick Finlay

It must be very hard for you, but I'm sure the Lord will give you a special love for the baby, even in the womb, and that in time to come, you will be able to give thanks, even if you don't understand.
Malcolm Duff

In May, many people got in touch by letter or phone to send us their love and tell us of their prayers for you.
Meanwhile, Dad and I were busy. We had just begun a weekly youth club in the church called 'Starters' and that was held each Friday night. I was busy at the State Hospital, trying to get all my work tidied up so that I could finish on 1st June with a clear conscience.
People in our evening service prayed for you, and when we went to visit our friends, John and Anne Collard, they prayed for you too.
Jennifer's Diary, May 1993

Amazingly, as John Collard preceded Gordon as minister of our current church in East Kilbride, that prayer took place in the house we now live in, which has made it an extra special family house for us – and given me a clear and distinct memory of Jennifer (before birth) being in this very room where I'm writing!

Preparing

Tragedies concerning babies had not been so openly talked about a few decades before. My youngest brother, Keith John Taylor, had died at the age of three months in 1967, when I was six years old. He had been very ill in hospital for some days but my mother was not allowed to sit where he could see her face, and was not allowed to hold him, even in death. When she returned home from that last hospital visit, my father and a family friend, with the best of intentions, had cleared every memory of Keith out of the house – cot, clothes, the lot. My mother was 'like a madwoman', upturning laundry baskets, emptying drawers, searching frantically for any trace of her son – anything tangible she could hold on to of her precious boy.

She found a teddy and a hairbrush. He was her fourth child and there were only two photographs of him. Keith's funeral was a burial, and at that time, in Scotland, it was customary for women not to attend funerals of any kind. She was a minister's wife, as well as a mother of three other young children, and she was expected to take up the mantle of chairing women's meetings again immediately.

Desperate that I should be spared these additional hurts, my mother had useful advice about preparation for our own baby's death and the funeral. I was also grateful to be able to talk with a colleague whose baby had died aged two weeks, and a friend who had had a late miscarriage, finding out what had helped them, and what they wished they had done differently at their time of loss.

I bought *When the Dream is Shattered*,[7] a manual for those suffering baby loss written by an Australian couple, but the more I read about the death of a baby, the more the little person inside me kicked, as if claiming my attention over those morbid thoughts. How could I read about grief with all that life and energy still bouncing around inside me?

It was important to have some idea of how we wanted things to be, however, as, if our baby died before twenty-six weeks, its loss would be termed a 'miscarriage'. If we were not ready to speak out, decisions about the disposal of its body might be made without us. Passing the milestone of twenty-six weeks, when our child's death would now be termed a stillbirth, there was relief in knowing that the hospital and authorities would acknowledge her life and deal with her death accordingly. At twenty-five weeks, a further scan had shown that our baby was very likely, but not definitely, a girl.

---

[7] Judith and Michael Murray, *When the Dream is Shattered: Coping with Child-bearing Difficulties* (Adelaide: Lutheran Publishing House, 1988).

My last day at the State Hospital was
1st June. I was sad to leave in some ways
– however, you were getting heavier and
the walk from our office to the wards was
getting more and more tiring, so it was
also quite a relief! The next day Dad and
I got ready and picked up his mum,
Gran Palmer, and we drove down to
Manchester. Dad was meeting up with
some of his pals to watch the Test Match
(cricket) of England v Australia, and
Gran came along to keep me company.
On Saturday, Gran got the bus back to
East Kilbride, and Dad and I travelled to
a little place called Crewe by Farndon. It
was very near Chester and on the
Sunday afternoon and evening we
explored the city, eating in an Italian
restaurant. There they provided crayons
for every table so that while we were
waiting for our food we could 'doodle' on
the paper tablecloth. So, I drew something
for you!
Jennifer's Diary, June 1993

"Woosh on the Wall"

While on holiday, I had thought Gordon and I should discuss how best to prepare for our baby's death – but he didn't want to. He said that while she was still with us, he wanted to enjoy her company and not talk about her death. Wise words, which transformed the pregnancy and our memories of it. We enjoyed everything and everywhere more, knowing that she was with us. We took more photographs of my pregnant shape.

The rest of the holiday was very relaxing. It was nice to know all the time that you were with us while we were enjoying ourselves. You certainly didn't let me forget, as your kicks were often very strong!

Back at our own church service in the evening, people prayed with us for you, knowing that God is able to care for you in lots of ways that none of the rest of us can.

Jennifer's Diary, June 1993

Help

Continuing with the pregnancy wasn't easy. Every pain made me anxious that I was going to miscarry. I had nightmares about what our baby might look like. Well-meaning strangers were forever asking if I wanted a boy or a girl, or if I was excited, and even some people who knew found it hard to believe the extent of the problems and would say something along the lines of, 'I'm sure everything will be fine.' Some would chide me for not knitting baby clothes or doing anything else to prepare for the birth. Others hushed it up, not telling mutual acquaintances or friends, which left us to field all the standard questions of, 'When's it due?' and, 'Have you got everything ready?' and to be the ones offering words of comfort when our situation was explained.

Some people tried to keep me away from small children. I'm sure it was with a desire to protect my feelings, but the result was that I was made to feel even more excluded from that world; not worthy to be a mother. I think, perhaps, any mother of an 'abnormal' child feels that there's something wrong with her that has made this child the way it is, so not letting her hold a small baby can make it feel as though the world agrees.

Overwhelmingly, however, our experience was of receiving tremendous help and support. I was wary about being on my own, but friends and family made sure I never was, and we knew that many people were praying for us every day. One man in our church, who had been an alcoholic, used to write a prayer for us every night and put it under his pillow.

The child no doubt is as much aware of your love and care as it is of any discomfort.
Margaret Masson

Be assured of my continual prayers.
Netty Sinclair

We do not know the answer to the 'whys' but we know that our Father is Almighty God who loves us. We do pray for you, especially Karen to experience God's special care.
Kornel and Anna Herjeczki

Just to say that you are in my thoughts and prayers every day – at all sorts of times you come to mind and when you do, I just ask the Lord to wrap His love around you both at that very moment.
Renee Johnstone

God brought you to my mind today as he does every day.
Grace Barclay

Janet Robertson[8] was bridesmaid at our wedding and has always been a really good friend. Over the month of July, she visited us frequently (usually late at night) and kept us in supplies of roses, rhubarb and Mars Bars!
Jennifer's Diary, July 1993

Janet's catchphrase was, 'I was just passing!' and the Mars Bars were for Gordon and arranged in bouquets.

On at least one occasion, I was far less gracious about accepting help than I should have been. My father, Jim Taylor, was a Baptist minister and my parents lived in a lovely, old, spacious manse in Stirling. A friend of mine who was passing through that area was keen to meet up with me, and so my mother offered the use of her lounge. 'Bring all your ironing for me to do,' she urged me, knowing what a huge pile of it I always had. I duly complied, taking it with me in the car, but when I arrived, although she pleaded with me, I was contrary and refused to take it out of the boot.

After my friend left, I went looking for Mum and found her in tears, in the kitchen. 'You're not a very good psychiatrist,' was her rebuke! And so I learned that

---

[8] Janet Robertson (27th January 1962–18th October 2012), a former flatmate of mine, was a GP in Moffat, in the Scottish borders. She died too soon, and is greatly missed by family, colleagues, patients, by those who, like me, considered her their best friend, and by many children, like our own, who loved her like an aunt.

sometimes we need to accept help, for the other person's sake – particularly when the other person is a loved one who feels otherwise helpless.

Hope

There were times when I was angry with our baby. At first, on the Monday of the first scan, I was angry with it for having ousted our normal child. Occasionally, I felt angry that this pregnancy was keeping us back from starting a 'proper' family. The angriest was three weeks after our holiday, when, thirty-three weeks pregnant, a scan showed only a tiny rim of lung tissue and the prognosis was grim. She was breech and unlikely to be able to turn owing to the lack of amniotic fluid. Vaginal delivery was likely to damage her further; the lack of fluid would compound the difficulty of giving birth to a bottom-first baby.

At an appointment with Dr Matthew, the question of Caesarean section arose. His preference was for vaginal delivery as he didn't think it was worth risking my health (even though the risks of Caesarean section are small) for such little gain. Our baby, even if she were to be born alive, was not expected to live long. I knew that putting this child first meant I should have a section, but I was angry at the futility of it. How much was I to sacrifice, for her to die anyway? What if the section made future deliveries hazardous?

The night after that appointment was the first night I lost substantial sleep, and I cried into a mug of tea in the early hours of the morning. That was the time it was hardest to love her.

We opted for a Caesarean section, and that decision brought an unexpected benefit. With the increased likelihood that our baby would be delivered alive came the need to discuss resuscitation, should she struggle to breathe on her own, and therefore I was given an appointment with Dr Al-Roomi, a consultant paediatrician. Dr Al-Roomi asked for my whole story from the very beginning and, as I spoke, she cried with me. She expressed real concern for our baby and I realised that she was the first member of staff to do so, even though everyone had given great care to Gordon and to me. She affirmed our decision to have a Caesarean section and give our baby the best chance possible – after all, she said, we didn't have a diagnosis and the ultrasound might have made the situation look worse than it actually was. She said that Gordon and I must have a tour of the Special Care Baby Unit (SCaBU) – a suggestion that seemed, at the time, like a flight of fancy, but I was enjoying it. Dr Al-Roomi gave me hope, which was what I needed at that time to love our little baby. It was too hard to love her fully without a little bit of hope, and so God, in His graciousness, gave me some.

On the 8th July I went to hospital and met a lovely lady called Dr Al-Roomi who is a paediatrician. She was very interested to hear all about you and said that she would like to be there on the day that you are born.

Jennifer's Diary, July 1993

Thanks for your card and the more helpful news you have shared therein. It's wonderful to have your own leanings at last confirmed. I'm so glad your baby is being acknowledged now as someone to be taken care of. May you know lots more of God's interference on your behalf.
Sue and Patrick Finlay

It was good to hear of the interview with the paediatrician. What an encouragement that must have been, and confirmation of your own thinking. Bless her heart! No wonder you felt different after seeing her.
Letter from Helen Taylor (my mother)

On the 25th July, I led our evening service, with 'Peace' as the theme, using some of what I had learned over all those weeks since the scan on Easter Monday. This was the talk I gave:

Often, powerful people like to instil fear in others and enjoy keeping them in their place. Not God.

Even at the beginning of the New Testament in Luke chapter 1, when an angel visits Zechariah, then Mary, he quickly says to them, 'Don't be afraid.'

The angels who came to the shepherds were bringing a message of 'peace with God' – but they also were conscious that their appearance might frighten the shepherds, so only one appeared first, with the message, 'Don't be afraid' – basically, 'There's going to be a whole army of us here in a minute, but we've come with good news!'

God doesn't want us to be frightened or afraid. That's easier said than done – without peace, our minds can run riot. In John's Gospel, chapter 14, Jesus tells the disciples that He is leaving them with a gift of peace. He says He's not giving them peace in the way the world does – 'Go in peace' and 'Peace be with you' were common enough greetings – but Jesus says He's leaving them with more than that – His own peace, that grows in us, as we allow the Holy Spirit to work.

But Jesus also issues a command. In verse 27 He also says, 'Do not let your hearts be troubled and do not be afraid.'[9] It's not a gift that you leave lying around in a drawer and do nothing about. We have to work with it ourselves. Well, how?

I think Jesus answers this in the last few verses of the chapter. He continues to talk about leaving them – which was a potentially frightening prospect for Him too as He was facing harsh beatings and a horrible death. But He talks about His trust in the Father, and His belief that Satan has no power over Him – He demonstrates that peace of mind and heart comes from trusting in God's promises.

Look at all the promises He gave the disciples in this chapter – there are more than ten amazing promises in it. He wasn't expecting them to stop being frightened by some kind of magic – but He wanted them to trust Him, that His promises are true.

In the same way, as we accept Christ's gift of peace, we can look at His promises and start believing them for ourselves.

---

[9] NIV.

Arrival – 'A Day of Unexpected Grace'

My due date was only a few weeks away and I didn't yet have a date for the section.

A few days later, the 29th July, was Gordon's birthday. The caption inside the card I gave him read, 'Wishing you a birthday of unexpected grace.' Little did either of us know that in more than one way, within the next week, that wish would be fulfilled.

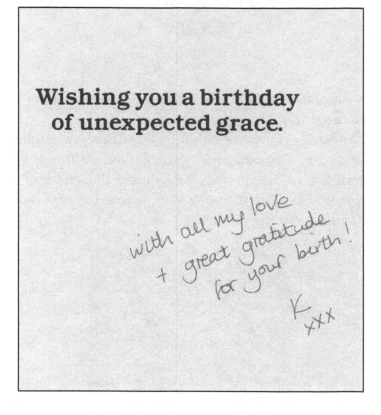

**Wishing you a birthday
of unexpected grace.**

with all my love
+ great gratitude
for your birth!

K
xxx

'Woosh-woosh' is poking and jabbing me under the ribs these days so still seems to have a reasonable amount of room. I'm sorry we don't have a date to give you as yet – Dr Matthew sounded busy when I phoned yesterday and when I think of how much we appreciated all the uninterrupted time he spent with us, I didn't want to keep him back from whatever he was doing or whoever he was seeing. He probably wasn't aware we had opted for the section as he'd got it into his head that we were non-interventionists – which I suppose would explain all our decisions up until this one. I catch myself getting excited about the delivery too but still shrivel a bit inside when someone says, 'And when's the big day?' And sometimes too it seems selfish to be longing for a date as that date might well be WW's last day with us. However – you have no idea how many people are praying for us – an astronomical number, and people we've never even met, so I'm certain we will all be palpably aware of that on the day.
Letter to my parents

The day after that was quite exciting because we went to hospital and were given YOUR birthday. We were told it was to be Tuesday 3rd August at approximately 9am – first on the list. That is the same birthday as Grandpa Taylor's father who, like Grandpa, was also called James Taylor.

The first day in August was a Sunday. People knew by now when you were to be born and, as Janet Anderson was doing the prayer for others, she prayed especially for the three of us. She asked all the congregation to read a passage out loud as a special prayer for you and Dad and Mum:

We ask God from the wealth of his glory
to give you power through his Spirit to be
strong in your inner selves, and *we* pray
that Christ will make his home in your
hearts through faith. *We* pray that you
may have your roots and foundation in
love, so that you, together with all God's
people, may have the power to understand
how broad and long, how high and deep,
is Christ's love. Yes, may you come to
know his love – although it can never be
fully known – and so be completely
filled with the very nature of God.
Ephesians 3:16-19[10]

---

[10] My italics. Janet asked the congregation to use 'we' instead of Paul's 'I'.

I think you must have known that you were being talked about, because you gave a great big punch in the air towards the end of the prayer as if to say, 'That's right! God loves me!'

The next day, Monday, I went into hospital, so that the doctors and nurses could get me ready for you to be born. Someone came with a cardiotocograph (CTG) – a monitor that they place on the mummy's tummy so that they can get a tracing of the baby's heartbeat and a tracing of any contractions the mum has. That lets them know how well the baby is coping with being squeezed. The mum also has to press a little button every time she feels a movement – and that gets recorded with the other tracings.

Well – you really played to the audience!
You kicked and punched and wriggled
like nobody's business. And the
accelerations in your heartbeat showed
that you were coping very well with
being squeezed – so I was very proud of
you. From that time on, on the Monday,
you kept your mum company – all
evening and all night I felt your little
nudges and prods. I didn't want to go to
sleep because I was enjoying it so much,
and didn't want to miss any of it. So –
for a little time, I sat out in the corridor
and read through all the letters that
people had sent us over the last months –
all the good wishes for the three of us,
and all the promises of God's love and
care.

Jennifer's Diary, August 1993

There were times towards the end when I would have rather the pregnancy could continue indefinitely than conclude with the loss of our precious child. I wished that I could carry her inside me, alive and kicking, forever.

On the morning of 3rd August, Dr Matthew performed an elective Caesarean section under spinal anaesthetic. The first we knew of our new arrival was when the green sheet was unpegged and he held her forward. And there was Jennifer – a pink, squirming, beautiful baby. Gordon and I were struck motionless in amazement. 'Come on,' smiled Dr Matthew, 'touch her – it's your turn before the paediatricians take her away.' We tasted real joy. We had a baby. I hadn't really expected a baby.

When people asked at the start of the pregnancy if I wanted a boy or a girl, I used to say, 'A baby.' That first scan, and my textbooks, medical friends and GP all prepared us for something that might not look much like a baby. I had two dreams. In one, they had delivered our child in hospital and wrapped it up in green towels before I could see it. I demanded to see it, and it looked like ET. I cuddled it, and it glowed like ET and came alive. It grew into an old man, who told us how grateful he was to us for loving him, and fascinated everyone with his stories of adventure and travel. In another dream, our child was lying sideways in a cot, its skull bossed and ugly. It looked at me with a knowing, penetrating look but I had to turn my eyes away. I did look back at it again, but felt so guilty and ashamed for that moment in which I had looked away. But God did give us a baby. Her cries were a baby's cries. I had to admit to being very surprised!

We were worried that we would never meet you, touch you, hold you. We are so glad that we did. You looked so peaceful and so beautiful. We heard you cry, we saw you kick, we felt you grasp.
Gordon's tribute

We could hear you cry – not that you sounded distressed – probably just a bit bemused and disorientated, having been dragged out into the big wide world so rapidly! When they were ready to take you to the Special Care Baby Unit, they wheeled you slowly past our heads so we could see you again. You looked lovely. We were so happy to see you and looked forward to when they would have sewn my tummy up and we could get to see you again.

We had chosen 'Jennifer' for you a long time before because it was such a pretty name, but we could not use it before you were born because we did not know for definite that you were a wee girl. We felt that you were – almost from the beginning (which is why this story was started in such a pretty book; just as well you weren't a boy – he would have been scandalised!).

'Grace', your middle name, came from God's grace which had been strengthening all three of us, and also from an elderly widow in our church, Grace Barclay. She has always been very good to your mum and dad. When she knew you were coming, she gave us gifts for you, including a lovely soft white towel. After she heard you were sick, she prayed for us all every day, and wrote little notes to encourage us. Poor Dad didn't get much choice in your middle name – apparently, I announced it as a fait accompli as you were handed to the paediatricians and then asked him if that was OK! He couldn't really have said no at that stage!

Jennifer's Diary, August 1993

After theatre I was wheeled along to a little single room in Recovery where I had a morphine syringe driver which I was able to have some control of myself. Neither excruciating pain nor sleep seemed like useful options, however, when I had a daughter to get fit for.

After you had been in SCaBU for about half an hour, Dad got to visit you. You were in your little incubator at the furthest-away part of the department, beside the window. He was very glad to see you again, and had a good look at his little daughter. You had a little tube in your mouth to help you breathe and little sticky pads so that a machine could give a tracing of your heartbeat.

Your next visitors were your two grandmas as Dad brought them to see you. They were delighted to watch you kicking, and they came and told me how beautiful you were. Then your two granddads visited you. You were kicking and kicking, and Grandpa Palmer said you looked like a real wee fighter!
Jennifer's Diary, August 1993

At this point, there was a communication blip, which was nobody's fault, and which, at least, caused a happy hiatus. One of the paediatricians came to find Gordon and me in Recovery and gave us the good news that things were not nearly as bad as had been feared. None of Jennifer's problems were life-threatening but she did have a cleft palate and a defect in her lower bowel and would need surgery to correct these. She was going to live!

Gordon went to let the grandparents know and, furnished with this exciting news, my parents went off to look at prams, after which my father returned to Stirling for a church meeting he hadn't expected to be able to attend.

Then Dad came to get me. It was now three and a half hours since you had been born so I was very pleased to see you at last. He wheeled me along to your incubator and there you were – lying on your right side and looking very sleepy. Your left eye was half-open and you were very peaceful. I thought maybe the doctors had given you medicine to make you sleepy but they said they hadn't. There were two portholes on the side of the incubator which we could open and then we were able to touch you. I could stroke your little tiny soft hand and see your little fingers curl round.
Jennifer's Diary, August 1993

We had prayed that she would be peaceful and comfortable, and she was. As a bonus, she was beautiful! There was little sign that the lack of fluid round about her had caused any discomfort. All four limbs moved well, and the hand that had appeared useless and 'clawed' on the scan grasped mine as she lay in the incubator. Her beauty and her straight and mobile limbs were proof that God had answered our prayers. She didn't look squashed. She had kicked so much in the pregnancy that sometimes it seemed she might burst her way out, and Dr Matthew was amazed that she was able to move so much despite so little amniotic fluid. I'm certain it was God taking care of her. I did and do wonder if we should have asked God to heal her. Others asked. I told God He could do it if He wanted to – I knew He could. I asked for a little miracle on the day. The fact that we saw her born alive and beautiful, and all the grandparents saw 'a real wee fighter' in the incubator was certainly a miracle.

The doctor attending Jennifer in SCaBU had given us a little time on our own beside her incubator. Now he came over to stand beside us. He told us that we had some decisions to make and I remember thinking, with excitement as well as trepidation, 'Here we go – this is the beginning of us looking after our little girl.' Out loud, I asked, 'You mean about surgery?' and watched as confusion then dismay filled his face.

Very gently, he explained the situation. A scan had confirmed that Jennifer had very little kidney tissue, and because the blood vessels needed for kidney function had not formed either, transplant was not an option. Fluid circulating as a baby develops in the womb helps to form the lungs, and so Jennifer only had tiny rims of lung tissue which were too fragile to ventilate for long. She could not survive, in any case, without kidneys. He told us that the ventilator had to be switched off as there was a serious risk of injuring what little lung tissue there was, which would be painful and distressing for her and would result in her dying very quickly. And so, we were spared that final decision.

Dad and I waited in a little room while the doctors took off all the sticky pads and tubes. Then the doctor brought you to us. It was so lovely to hold you. You were our little treasure! Both of us held you and were able to have several minutes saying hello to you before we had to say goodbye. You were very peaceful. Both your eyes were closed and you made a little snuffly noise now and again, screwing your nose up. Dad held your hand, and you went straight from our arms into the Father's arms. We still had your precious little body but we knew already that you were safe with Him, cosy and cuddled and whole.
Jennifer's Diary, August 1993

It was only as I put this book together and worked on the chronology that I realised there was a gap in my knowledge here. And so, twenty-six years later, I asked Gordon if he remembered. Of course he remembered. He it was who had to go back to the room where his parents were, breaking down in tears as he told them the news, and then search for my mother.

Gran and Grandpa Palmer then came and saw how beautiful you had been. Then Grandma Taylor came. We took some photographs to help us remember and dressed your little body in a sleepsuit. Your little hands and feet were so soft and so sweet! We had to roll the sleeves of the sleepsuit up, and your feet only went half way down its legs! Then we cooried[11] your body in Grace's lovely soft towel and tucked a little teddy bear in the folds. We had a hat for you, but didn't want to put it on as it would have hidden your gorgeous hair, which was dark with reddish tints and even curly on top! Then a nurse took you away and we left SCaBU. They brought your body back for us later on so that we could see

---

[11] A Scottish word implying, in this context, 'lovingly swaddled'.

again how sweet and beautiful you had been, but all the time we knew that you were somewhere much better.
Jennifer's Diary, August 1993

In many of the photographs we took we are smiling because, even then, while we felt so sad, we also felt grateful for her life and bowled over with how beautiful she was. Her nose was a bit squint and snubbed and gave her quite a snooty appearance (like my dad, we joked). Her little ears were pressed back against the sides of her head, but other than that, there were no obvious signs of her having spent so long in such a confined space.

Imagine for a moment what it was like for my mother to hold Jennifer and to help dress her, having been denied those sacred tasks so many years before when her own son had died. There was healing for her in those last moments of caring for her granddaughter. She moved away to talk with Dr Matthew and some of the other staff, and I could hear her speaking about her little Keith. To have them listen to her story was also a help to her. Her mother's heart was soothed by having a lost son acknowledged, and seeing first-hand that protocols had changed in time for her daughter to have a completely different experience. Even in death, God used Jennifer to bless.

At Rottenrow in August 1993, ward accommodation for bereaved mothers was pretty good but had been hard won. A little room in the labour suite had been funded by donations, following the sad death of a midwife's baby. I benefited from that little oasis for two nights, but then had to vacate it for someone else who, tragically, was in a similar situation.

These were still the days when an inpatient stay after a Caesarean section was typically four or five nights.

I spent the next couple of nights in a single room, just outside the postnatal ward. I could hear babies crying and, particularly at night, when I knew staff would be looking after the babies to let mums have a sleep (that luxury happened too!), I was so tempted to tiptoe through and ask to hold one for a while. All of my heart and mind was crying out for my baby and my body was crying out too, with hormones sending milk that leaked onto my clothes. But I didn't tiptoe through, and I didn't ask, irrationally afraid that I might not be trusted – that the 'real' mothers would be scared in case I might flee with their child, or drop it just for spite.

As any exhausted junior doctor or long-term patient knows, hospital cleaners and their kindnesses can be a lifeline. Life experience or natural intuition told them that the woman in the side room would not be sleeping well, and so my door pushed open in the early hours of each morning with offers of cups of tea. Blessings upon them.

And then it was time to go home – but I had a problem: my room resembled a florist's shop! The solution came with a phrase that popped, fully formed, into my head: 'Everywhere she had been there grew flowers.' We tried to think if it came from some novel or poem. With the advent of Google some years later, I hunted for it with no joy. Maybe you, lovely reader, know the source, and if so, let me know! But at the moment, I have to consider the possibility that God gave it to me – for a purpose and a promise.

First the purpose…

There were so many flowers sent to us in the hospital that by the time I was ready to go home, there were enough to go everywhere in the hospital that had something to do with you – the place where we went to see you on the ultrasound scan, and where we talked to Dr Matthew about you, and SCaBU. So now, when your mum sees pretty and delicate flowers, she thinks of you, and imagines that other people do too!
Jennifer's Diary, August 1993

The display of flowers in my little side room was certainly a thing of wonder. Friends had chosen carefully. It being the height of summer, some were garden posies, many had arrived in bud and there was a lovely bunch of fragrant lavender. Sitting among the blooms, a photo frame holding a SCaBU polaroid of Jennifer had a miniature rose attached to it with surgical tape.

All packed, with plenty of time to spare before Gordon would arrive to take me home, I worked my way round the various departments, leaving a blessing of flowers everywhere Jennifer had been.

To read about the fulfilment of the promise, you'll need to wait until later...

Home

In some ways, Ruchazie was not the easiest place to return to. We didn't live in a large or comfortable manse, but a third-floor flat, in what in Glasgow is called a 'close'. Many in our housing scheme faced enormous challenges on a daily basis; substance misuse was widespread and violent incidents were not unusual. We were among many who had to endure the stress of a noisy neighbour and, during the lighter evenings of summer, mass fights would occur between young people from Ruchazie and the neighbouring housing scheme of Cranhill, on the motorway bridge outside our block.

We had discovered early on, however, that one consequence of all of those issues was a lack of social veneer. Conversations couldn't skate upon the safe surface of chat about work, because there often was no work; instead, they quickly plunged deeper into conversations about family and home life. Glaswegians are well known for their lack of reserve, but Ruchazie was a step beyond that! For any journey on foot around the scheme, extra allowance always had to be made for bumping into people who would ask, even if they didn't know us, where we were off to or what we were doing. We enjoyed that, recognising genuine friendliness and interest rather than nosiness.

Another consequence was that many had expertise in facing tragedy, and it was humbling to discover ourselves ministered to by other residents in our time of grief. A young woman who had experienced multiple miscarriages visited in order to share very practical advice about how she had learned to cope following her own losses. A few visitors – including some nuns who lived locally – visited out of concern for us, but said and asked nothing about our baby.

That was in marked contrast to some younger, indigenous callers! Three little brothers, Derek, Darren and Jimmy, prior to Jennifer's birth had visited regularly for hot chocolate, to watch *Mr Bean* videos and to play with Duplo and Lego. They had been touchingly concerned for me ever since Easter, when we had told them about our baby's problems. When they knew we were back in residence, the brothers reappeared at our house with one of their cousins, Elaine. They carefully examined the framed photograph of Jennifer, and when, on another visit, they brought two more cousins – Karen and Bryan – the photo was part of their tour of the house. They were helpfully matter of fact about it all. When Elaine told Karen that the photo was of my baby who had died, Karen, aged nine, asked what we had called her, and when I replied, 'Jennifer,' she said, 'That's a pretty name.' Such an ordinary question and comment; yet, what comfort! Like any new mum, all I wanted to do was talk about my little one.

I ached for my lost child. As a result, I craved children being around me, so what pleasure when those same brothers and a cousin or two all piled in beside me at our church service on Sunday morning! Sadly, a well-meaning member shooed them all out of the pew again and took them to sit with the other children at the front.

Letting Go

PALMER — At Rottenrow Maternity on Tuesday, 3rd August, 1993, JENNIFER GRACE, daughter of Gordon and Karen nee Taylor. Funeral Services at Ruchazie Parish Church, Elibank St., on Monday, 9th August, at 12.30pm, funeral thereafter to Riddrie Park Cemetery, all relatives and friends are welcome.

Back at home, our focus as a couple had become the preparations for Jennifer's funeral. Again, we looked to John Bell's words which resonated so much with the confusion of grief we were experiencing. We wanted again to use his responsive readings in order to let everyone attending the funeral feel involved, and we wanted some of the responses and readings to be those that God had used so powerfully during Holy Week.

One of John's hymns which spoke helpfully into our pain was 'The Love of God Comes Close', but it was a Communion hymn, and Communion is not generally celebrated at Protestant funerals. We altered it slightly, substituting our own words for the verse about the bread and wine. There was not time to ask John's permission, but I wrote to him to let him know and to thank him for all the help his words had been to the people of Ruchazie church and to ourselves, particularly in the months leading up to Jennifer's birth.

JENNIFER GRACE PALMER
3rd August 1993

Opening Responses:
Leader: God is our shelter and strength, always
ready to help in times of trouble.
All: The Lord Almighty is with us!
Leader: When we are afraid he comforts us.
All: The Lord Almighty is with us!
Leader: When we are sad he brings us joy.
All: The Lord Almighty is with us!
Leader: God is always with us and he cannot be
defeated.
All: The Lord Almighty is with us!
Leader: Who is with us?
All: The Lord Almighty is with us!
Leader: Will he ever leave us?
All: No!
Leader: The Lord Almighty is with us! He reigns
supreme for ever!
All: Hallelujah!

The Saviour died but rose again
Triumphant from the grave;
And pleads our cause at God's right hand
Omnipotent to save.

Who then can e'er divide us more
From Jesus and his love,
Or break the sacred chain that binds
The earth to heaven above?

Let troubles rise, and terrors frown
And days of darkness fall;
Through him all dangers we'll defy,
And more than conquer all

Nor death, nor life, nor earth, nor hell
Nor time's destroying sway,
Can e'er efface us from his heart
Or make his love decay.

Each future period that will bless,
As it has blessed the past;
He loved us from the first of time
He loves us to the last.

****　　****　　****　　****　　****

We cannot measure how you heal
Or answer every sufferer's prayer,
Yet we believe your grace responds
Where faith and doubt unite to care.

Your hands though bloodied on the cross,
Survive to hold and heal and warn,
To carry all through death to life
And cradle children yet unborn.

The pain that will not go away,
The guilt that clings from things long past,
The fear of what the future holds,
Are present as if meant to last.

But present too is love which tends
The hurt we never hoped to find,
The private agonies inside,
The memories that haunt the mind.

So some have come who need your help
And some have come to make amends,
As hands which shaped and saved the world
Are present in the touch of friends.

Lord, let your Spirit meet us here
To mend the body, mind and soul,
To disentangle peace from pain
And make your broken people whole.

****　　****　　****　　****　　****

The love of God comes close
where stands an open door
to let the stranger in,
to mingle rich and poor:
the love of God is here to stay
embracing those who walk his way.

The peace of God comes close
to those caught in the storm,
forgoing lives of ease
to ease the lives forlorn:
the peace of God is here to stay
embracing those who walk his way.

The joy of God comes close
where faith encounters fears,
where heights and depths of life
are found through smiles and tears:
the joy of God is here to stay
embracing those who walk his way.

The grace of God comes close
to those whose grace is spent,
when hearts are tired or sore
and hope is bruised or bent:
the grace of God is here to stay
embracing those who walk his way.

The Son of God comes close
to heal and to forgive,
he gives his life to us
that we in him might live:
the Son of God is here to stay
embracing those who walk his way.

Closing Responses:
Leader: The desert will sing and rejoice
All   : And the wilderness blossom with flowers
Leader: All will see the Lord's splendour
All   : See the Lord's greatness and power
Leader: Tell everyone who is anxious
All   : Be strong and don't be afraid
Leader: The blind will be able to see
All   : The deaf will be able to hear
Leader: The lame will leap and dance
All   : Those who can't speak will shout
Leader: This is the promise of the Lord
All   : His promise will be fulfilled.

Gordon, during the early days of bereavement, had found the book *Lament for a Son* by Nicholas Wolterstorff to be hugely helpful. It took the form of a diary which Wolterstorff had kept during the days, weeks and months after his twenty-five-year-old son was killed in a mountaineering accident. Gordon asked his good friend Jim Reid to read an excerpt at the funeral – one which had helped him to make some sense of what we were going through:

> 'Put your hands into my wounds,' said the risen Jesus to Thomas, 'and you will know who I am.' The wounds of Christ are his identity. They tell us who he is. He did not lose them. They went down in to the grave with him and they came up with him – visible, tangible, palpable. Rising did not remove them. He who broke the bonds of death kept his wounds.
>
> To believe in Christ's rising from the grave is to accept it as a sign of our own rising from our graves. If for each of us it was our destiny to be obliterated, and for all of us together it was our destiny to fade away without a trace, then not Christ's rising but my son's early dying would be the logo of our fate.
>
> Slowly I begin to see that there is something more as well. To believe in Christ's rising and death's dying is also to live with the power and the challenge to rise up now from all our dark graves of suffering love. If sympathy for the world's wounds is not enlarged by our anguish, if love for those around us is not expanded, if gratitude for what is good does not flame up, if

insight is not deepened, if commitment to what is important is not strengthened, if aching for a new day is not intensified, if hope is weakened and faith diminished, if from the experience of death comes nothing good, then death has won. Then death, be proud.

So, I shall struggle to live the reality of Christ's rising and death's dying. In my living, my dear son's early dying will not be the last word. But as I rise up, I bear the wounds of his death. My rising does not remove them. They mark me. If you want to know who I am, put your hand in.[12]

Jennifer's little body was buried high on a hill in Riddrie Park Cemetery, a short drive from Ruchazie, but a long walk. My memories of the service there are vague. Alistair again leading, Gordon rubbing my back as we stood, a lady from Ruchazie church and her sister supporting each other as they wept. And the sudden realisation that we weren't the only parents bearing grief for a child that day.

---

[12] Wolterstorff, *Lament for a Son* (pp 92-93).

We had a special service in church to say thank you to God for you and to say goodbye to your little body. People came from hundreds of miles. There were more than 150 people altogether so, as one of them said – you had a lot of friends! At the start of the service, our friend, John Payne, played part of the *Messiah* on the piano. If we had sung the words for that part, they would have been, 'He shall feed his flocks like a shepherd and he shall gather the lambs with his arm.'[13] That reminded me of how gently God cared for you, and was still caring for you, and how tenderly He loved you. In fact, we sang in the service of how Jesus carries the unborn child in His arms – that was you! At the end of the service we all said together God's promise that in heaven we will be whole and complete.
Jennifer's Diary, August 1993

---

[13] Public domain.

It's hard to let go. But we have to – because where you are now, you are whole and complete and have much more room. Jennifer Grace: we look forward to meeting you again one day.
Gordon's tribute

Planned
Longed for
Created in love
Unseen
Cherished
'Jennifer Grace'
Our child
Gift of God
welcome.
A clasped finger
Lock of hair
Held
Adored
Let go..

from
Janet Anderson
+ the Sunday School

Just in case we had any doubt that you were safe, God arranged for a rainbow to encircle our house that evening, to remind us of that promise we had said together at the end of the service. He wanted us to be very certain that you were in good hands. He had known you very specially from the very beginning and had got your name written on the palm of His hand![14]
Jennifer's Diary, August 1993

In the days that followed, letters and cards arriving through our letter box were a continuing source of comfort and help. How thoughtfully and beautifully friends and relatives put words together – words that spoke to us and lifted us. They were brave and courageous, daring to put sentences together when it would have been easier not to. Often, those particular friends and family members had themselves come through significant losses.

Remembering Jennifer and being thankful for the love in which she was conceived the love by which she was carried and the love with which she was surrounded on her birthday.
Alistair and Su Drummond

You still have been a mum and dad even if it was for a short time. The gift of love was still yours to treasure forever.
A young woman from Ruchazie who had lost a child in a cot death

I understand from Karen's mum how much you have proved God's grace, and how graciously your prayers have been answered in specific ways.
Douglas Hutcheon, then superintendent of the Scottish Baptist Union

I'm so pleased that you had a short time to love her after her birth and I'm certain that she would have known that the love which surrounded her in utero continued and expanded during her tiny life.
Rosemary Luke, whose husband, Stewart (my mother's cousin), had died suddenly at the age of forty-eight

I know that Jennifer will be special to you in that she was part of both of you. I only have to look around and see Anne, my late wife, in members of our family, her features and her smile. You may also see likenesses in your future family.
Allan Cassidy, recently widowed

It was lovely being an auntie for even a short time. The sky was bluer and the world seemed full of hope and promise because of little Jennifer's life, short though it was.
Linda Taylor, my sister-in-law

Your little daughter Jennifer will always be part of your family and have a special place in it and in your lives and nothing can take that away.
Ruth Sinclair, a friend who had battled with post-natal depression

*It was lovely to see you here a few weeks ago, and I
hope it doesn't sound silly to say that I feel privileged
that Jennifer was also here.*
Ann Chester

*May you know the truth of these words of prophecy
spoken before the birth of another child:
'Our God is merciful and tender. He will cause the
bright dawn of salvation to rise on us and to shine from
heaven on all those who live in the dark shadow of
death, to guide our steps into the path of peace.' Luke
1:78-80*
Elliot Wardlaw

And then came a letter from Grace Barclay, who had been
such a support to us during the pregnancy – and with the
letter came a revelation…

*I felt highly honoured when I heard you had called the
baby Grace – it was a beautiful thought … Jennifer
Grace, a pretty name. I lost a wee baby too, Karen, he
was two months.*

Not once, while I was expecting Jennifer, had Grace told
us about the little boy she had lost. But now she could talk
about him with us, and his life and her grief for him could
be acknowledged. She wrote again to thank us for giving
her a photograph of Jennifer. We were catching another

glimpse of how God was using Jennifer as a comfort and help to others:

> *... she was the most beautiful baby, all the things you told me in your letter from the hospital I see in the picture. I bought a nice wee frame and have you all beside me in my bedroom ... I just want to say again how much I appreciate you naming your beautiful daughter Jennifer Grace. I feel when I look at her, she is part of me.*

Of course, no number of cards, letters, photographs and memories could make up for us not having Jennifer with us. There's something potentially materialistic about grief. Before she was born, anticipating her death, people and books had advised us to 'make memories', and, like most of the advice I was given, I had taken it. We took photographs, I finished her diary, I made a loose-leaf book of all the cards, letters, etc. I even kept pretty ribbons from a flower arrangement because they seemed like 'Jennifer' ribbons. I could sense the danger that all those things could crowd out the fragile memories I had of her and the danger that if something happened to the things – the book, the diary, the grave, the snowdrops we'd planted – I would feel like I'd lost her and not notice that fragile memory any more. The things were like a rosebush that would need regular pruning so that it could stay simple and beautiful, and not overgrow the real memory – that of a beautiful child being lifted out of me, and a little treasure in my arms.

A month after her birth, trying to sort out all the turmoil in my head, this poem formed:

I want to write a poem about you because you were so beautiful!
I felt humbled by your peaceful beauty
realising that such a beautiful and peaceful child
had been growing inside me
all these months!
These months – when I hadn't always felt peaceful,
when I'd been frightened of what you might look like
and so frightened that, with your death, might come relief,
when I hadn't always felt able to love you.
And now, your look of peace and beauty rebukes me
as if to say that you never doubted God was listening to us.
And I don't want to let go.
I grasp at all I have of you –
the photographs, cards and letters expressing people's care
and it's as if they all melt away
leaving me with nothing of you at all.
And yet, I'm glad that I miss you so much.
It would have been awful to have felt indifferent to your going.
This hurt is confirmation of your uniqueness and specialness.
It confirms my relationship with you.
No one will ever replace you.

The hole in our lives is Jennifer-shaped
and so, you can be seen in our lives
and will always be part of our family.

Gifts

September also brought a reply from John Bell, with a surprising and wonderful enclosure. He had written a song for us before even receiving my letter!

Dear Karen,

I read your letter today on returning from England and was profoundly touched by your kindness in writing and your encouragement.

The night before I went South, I spent a while with Doug Gay who told me how you had received Jennifer and given her back in a very short while. I was stunned and saddened to hear it and intended to write on my return.

As one who has never been near parenthood, I cannot claim any common ground with your experience. But marvellously in the Body of Christ we are compelled to empathise with what we do not understand and feel, for those whose lot is different.

It must surely have been a great consolation and witness to all around you that Gordon and you were responsible to Jennifer and loved her from this life into the next. There she will surely run and play and grow tall for the day when she welcomes her parents into heaven.

I wrote the enclosed on the train down to England. It came strangely quickly. The tune has not yet come, nor will I force it. But both will be for you and your family.

I remember you fondly in my prayers.

Every blessing

John

10th September 1993[15]

---

[15] Personal correspondence, used with kind permission.

A CRADLING SONG

We cannot care for you the way we wanted,
or cradle you or listen for your cry;
but, seperated as we are by silence,
love will not die.

We cannot watch you growing into childhood
and find a new uniqueness every day;
but special as you would have been among us,
you still will stay.

We cannot know the pain or the potential
which passing years would summon or reveal;
but for that true fulfilment Jesus promised
we hope and feel.

So, through the mess of anger, grief and tiredness,
through tensions which are not yet reconciled,
we give to God the worship of our sorrow
and our dear child.

Lord, in your arms which cradle all creation
we rest and place our baby beyond death,
believing that she, now alive in heaven,
breathes with your breath.

10 Sept '93

We wrote to thank John, and he wrote these words in reply: 'It is a great privilege for us to have found words which speak for others. And it is a greater joy to find how in all things God keeps his promise and all shall be well.'

Some years later, 'A Cradling Song' was included in the Iona community compilation, *When Grief is Raw*. The tune had come. To our great wonder, and the great delight of my father in particular, it was also included in the new volume of the Church of Scotland hymnary, CH4. And now the tune had a name: 'Jennifer'.

Flowers in the Wilderness

Two months after Jennifer's birth, I wrote in my diary that I was nearer to happiness than I had been since before her death and yet felt sadder than ever at the same time. Both feelings were very strong – a richness of feeling, very similar to that described in a poem I had written after getting to know her lovely dad on a summer mission ten years previously:

> What is it about people
> that when they have gone
> you are left richer
> but a little emptier
> through the experience?

Except that I felt much richer and much emptier.

Some comfort came at a Communion service which Gordon led. He explained that as we shared Communion together we also shared it with all the saints, and I realised that included Jennifer; not because Jennifer was a saint in the common understanding of the word, but because she was an infant child of believers and therefore covered by God's covenant to His Church.[16] When taking

---

[16] See 1 Corinthians 7:14.

Communion during the pregnancy, I had taken it for Jennifer too, claiming God's promises for her. After her death, Communion was hard because, once again, mine was the only body I was feeding with the bread and wine. But what Gordon said made me feel differently so that, from then on, I was again able to feel close to her during Communion. Communion would still be for me the remembrance of Christ's death, but I could remember it with her.

We travelled south for the wedding of a former Careforce worker in Ruchazie, Stephen Mawhinney, and, en route, stopped off in Durham to visit good friends there. News came that the death toll from a recent earthquake in Bombay had reached 10,000 – not families grieving for loved ones but loved ones grieving for families. I wondered, in the perspective of that, if perhaps I had no right to grieve for Jennifer. At that time, there was unimaginable horror in Bosnia and countless other places every day. On the scale of human misery and suffering, our experience hardly registered.

But then it dawned on me: the good news of our Christian faith is that each one of us is special and loved by God. To deny our grief for Jennifer would be to deny that she was valuable and precious, not just in our sight, but in God's. To deny our grief for her would be to let life be cheap, but it is not. Our grief for Jennifer wasn't negated by all those thousands of thousands of grieving people across the world – but we joined with them in our grief, and with God whose heart ached for each one.

In London, during the wedding ceremony, familiar words which described having, caring for and bringing up children as a purpose of marriage surprised me with their rebuke.

On our way home we went to a church service with the family of a young woman who was coming back with us to be our new Careforce volunteer. It was a prize-giving service for children in the congregation – couple after couple going forward with adorable babies and toddlers to collect books. It felt almost unbearable. 'First times' after a bereavement are probably always difficult; other weddings and other prize-givings would gradually become easier.

October also brought my birthday, and it felt sad to be saying goodbye to the age that I had been – thirty-two – when Jennifer was conceived, born and died, as if again I was losing part of her. But my thirty-third birthday was a Tuesday, and with the memory of Jennifer having been born on a Tuesday came the realisation that every year our birthdays would be on the same day of the week. I was – and am, year by year – so glad to have that extra bond. I was scared of forgetting her. I was also glad that I had a visible scar from the section as a reminder to me, and anyone who would ever have to physically examine me, that she had been real.

We had received word of a hospital follow-up appointment and were keen to find out if we had the green light to go ahead and try for another pregnancy. At the appointment, Dr Matthew told us that none of the tests performed (very limited in 1994) had revealed any genetic abnormality. It therefore looked as if Jennifer's condition was 'just one of those things' – a one-in-a-million event, extremely unlikely to recur. Going over the results, he disclosed that she had also had a small congenital heart defect which hadn't been picked up on the scans, and that made me feel so sorry for her. For someone so little, she had so many obstacles in the way of a healthy life. I also, irrationally, felt like a bad mother for not having known. Her gravestone had recently been erected in Riddrie cemetery, and so the day after the appointment I took up a bunch of pink rosebuds – a sort of 'sorry' for the heart defect.

Twelve days later, I was at the cemetery again, feeling bad at having stayed away so long, and not having brought fresh flowers. The weather was dull, wet and miserable, and I was rushing, but I was met with the most amazing sight! There, at the grave, were the most beautiful pink roses! They had blossomed! I remembered the responses we had said as a church on the Monday of Holy Week, and again at Jennifer's funeral – 'the wilderness will blossom with flowers.'*[17] God was reminding me that He can be totally trusted.

And that wasn't the end – three weeks later I returned, again expecting the flowers to be withered, but they were still beautiful, and frozen solid, on a rosy, pink day.

Intertwined with all the rose incidents had been a rather rocky return to work. I was returning not to the State Hospital, but to my base hospital, Parkhead in Glasgow. The consultant I was to be working under knew about Jennifer, as did other medical colleagues, but sadly, word had not spread widely, and all that some colleagues knew

---

[17] Responses written by WGRG which included these words from Isaiah 35:1-2.

was that I had been on maternity leave. As day one drew to a close, our unsuspecting social worker commented that I'd be keen to get home to my bouncing baby. Imagine his distress! Equally, the hospital's senior nurse who, a few weeks later, was walking along a corridor with me and asked how 'the wee one' was doing.

Life had also become increasingly unsettled for us in Ruchazie. Gordon was more and more convinced that the church would be better served by a new minister with fresh vision. Home life was more difficult too. For the last year or so, a neighbour had played music loudly in her house into the early hours every time she got drunk. As anyone who has suffered neighbour noise knows, it's not the kind of noise that you acclimatise to. Rather, you become sensitised, noticing the small signs leading up to it, finding your heart racing, dreading the hours ahead. Things had quietened after Jennifer's death, but quickly worsened again.

Grace Abounding

Just after Christmas, as I drove home from some grocery shopping, I noticed a familiar metallic taste in my mouth. A pregnancy kit from the chemists confirmed what I already suspected. Mixed in with the joy and excitement of the succeeding days, however, were other emotions. Guilt that I might be being disloyal to Jennifer, having got pregnant again so soon. Concern for this new child, that he/she might feel they had just been brought into being quickly as a substitute. I worried that friends might be shocked or disappointed in me, as if I'd treated Jennifer's death casually. In reality, one friend was rather hurt that I didn't tell her our good news until several more weeks had passed. I was almost surprised that people were happy for us. But it was God who had brought her/him into being – not us. And I did feel ready. I wanted this child, and welcomed it as a new, special, separate individual.

Much was changing for us as a couple. Gordon had applied to be minister of a congregation in Edinburgh and they duly elected him. I informed my consultant that I would be finishing work at the end of January, and also told him of the pregnancy. He had never said anything about Jennifer, but expressed delight at our news.

As I sat in the antenatal waiting area of Rottenrow for my first appointment, negotiating small talk was challenging. Glasgow deserves its reputation as a friendly city – strangers often chat easily to one another – but I struggled with how to answer the innocent enquiries of, 'Is this your first?' without causing upset. Dr Matthew came to my rescue, spotting me and whisking me away. Our planned move to Edinburgh made antenatal care a little more complicated, but he arranged for all my blood tests, and recommended Dr Luke, a colleague at Simpson Memorial Maternity Pavilion (SMMP). Best of all, he said that he would happily perform my detailed scan at eighteen weeks, even although by then we would have moved out of his area.

Landing in antenatal care in Edinburgh was bumpy. Discussing referral with our new GP, it made good practical sense to be seen by the local clinic rather than at SMMP, which was in the centre of the city. The obstetrician covering the local clinic was not Dr Luke, but the clinic had a well-organised system for first appointments, allowing patients to see all necessary disciplines within a short time. I was given an appointment very quickly, and, happily, Gordon was free to attend with me.

Disappointingly, the midwife knew nothing of our history. It seemed unlikely that the information would have been missing from the referral letter so perhaps she had just not had a chance to read it, with the clinic being so busy. Certainly, we appeared to wrong-foot her. Rather than express sympathy when we told her about Jennifer, she said we should not have arranged to have the eighteen-week scan in Glasgow as there were perfectly capable ultrasonographers locally. She also insisted on repeating all the recently performed blood tests. We were asked to wait to see the obstetrician, and although my notes had been handed through to him, again he was unaware that our first baby had died. Once more we explained. By the time we found ourselves giving our story a third time to a further member of staff, incredulity took over from my distress. The NHS I worked for was capable of being so much better.

By that time, we were already aware of the Stillbirth and Neonatal Death Society (SANDS). I knew of their teardrop stickers[18] which could be stuck on the front of case notes, alerting medical professionals to previous baby loss. I ordered some through the post, sent them to the clinic, and asked for my antenatal care to be transferred to Dr Luke's clinic at SMMP.

Pregnancy is an anxious time for many and was so for us. As the time grew closer for the detailed scan, I grew tense. I was doing locum work in Gogarburn, another long-stay hospital for patients with severe learning difficulties, many of whom had lived there since childhood, so that perhaps fuelled my anxieties once more. Some friends found it easier to be in touch now that we had good news to share. In my lowest moments I wondered if more bad news might make them turn from us in repulsion – maybe they would feel there was something wrong with us because God was not blessing us. Or perhaps those who had supported us so well during

---

[18] https://www.sands.org.uk/professionalsprofessional-resources/teardrop-stickers (accessed 14th May 2020).

the pregnancy with Jennifer would tire of us, and we would be left unsupported and alone. I was still haunted by the thought that I was a bad mother who harmed her children in the few weeks after conception.

During a baptism service, I sat worrying that we would never have a child who would live long enough to be baptised in the church building. I would waken in the night, feel the bump and decide it was too small, even though antenatal appointments were raising no concerns. On Mother's Day, I had the completely irrational thought that the midwives might just be humouring me because they knew the eighteen-week scan would tell me the awful truth soon enough. I wrestled in frustration with all those thoughts – hadn't I given that whole talk about peace in Ruchazie? But how could I trust God to look after this baby when He had let all that happen to Jennifer? I wasn't angry with God – I knew He'd been with us, and I knew that He had loved Jennifer and kept her comfortable. But if He had let Jennifer die, might He not let this baby die too? How could I have any sense of peace?

I knew that if the scan showed this baby to have the same problems, God would once more give us all that we needed to cope. But I dreaded the thought of going through it all again – for Gordon's and my sakes, but also for our parents. Peace only seemed possible, at that moment, if I could be certain that our child was well. That meant believing that God was both willing and able to make our baby well. I knew He was able, but was He willing? Surely, He would be willing. He loved our baby, and us and our parents – and He shared our sorrow over

Jennifer. 'If you want to,' I prayed, 'please make this baby well.'

I had a conversation about death and bereavement with Leonard Scott, a lovely retired minister in our church whose wife had died six years previously. All of my muddled thoughts seemed to fall away. Of course I could trust God completely – Holy Week in 1993 should have taught me that. I could be totally sure of His love for our baby and His desire for it to be well. He wasn't the one who harmed. God was the one who was with us and grieved our losses. He had already won victory over death. We and our child were totally safe and secure in His care, whatever the future held.

The day before the scan, I craved company and someone to talk to. Our wonderful friend Janet Robertson, who so often followed God's prompts, phoned that evening.

Fifty-three weeks after the ultrasound examination that had shown all of Jennifer's problems, in the very same scanning room, Dr Matthew was typically kind and thorough, checking everything down to numbers of fingers and toes. Everything was normal and he pronounced our baby a girl. From eighteen weeks of pregnancy, she was Ruth Joy. I was delighted that I wouldn't miss out on the joy of caring for and getting to know a daughter. I was aware of the dangers of looking for a substitute for Jennifer – but we had met Jennifer, and Ruth was a different child. For a start, her nose was a different shape, and we had scan photographs to prove it!

While in Glasgow, we visited Jennifer's grave, taking pink roses from Ruth. We arrived at a rare, sunny moment in the day, and about twenty beautiful little lilac crocuses had pushed through the earth around the headstone.

For a while after the scan, we felt reassured. Then, with this pregnancy, we began to experience something new – waiting! There had been no 'waiting' for Jennifer as far as I had been concerned. There had been for my mother, who had wished it all to be over for my sake; and other people had commented that the waiting must have been hard. But I hadn't waited for Jennifer like I waited for Ruth. Every day with Jennifer had been a bonus. We had appreciated time with the unborn Jennifer more than this time with the unborn Ruth, which I wanted to pass quickly so that she would be out, and I could see her and hold her and know she was OK without waiting for the next kick.

We didn't know Jennifer before she was born – didn't know she was a girl (though we suspected), didn't know she'd be beautiful, didn't know she'd look like a 'normal' baby. But all the love and prayers focusing on her during the pregnancy made her a person – a person damaged and incomplete, but loved. We were under no illusion with Jennifer – she wasn't an imaginary person. She was weak and vulnerable and needy. We knew and cared for her intimately, with that knowledge of her. Ruth, however, was the big unknown! I would find myself creeping back to that imaginary, idealised child whom we had lost the day of Jennifer's twenty-week scan – that child we had hoped and dreamed of, but who wasn't real. But if I took that image of Ruth away, I had nothing. I had no idea what she would be like, whereas we had had some ideas about Jennifer. Why should Ruth be any more like that imaginary child than Jennifer? We determined to love her, and knew that we would, no matter what.

We had never attended antenatal classes before and initially were thrilled to be part of normal preparation for a 'normal' birth. Rehearsals of delivery in the antenatal class were surprisingly upsetting, however. Every time I closed my eyes, I imagined that the child being lifted onto me was lifeless. The poor midwife leading the classes didn't know what to do with me.

I enjoyed getting things ready for a new daughter, but sometimes it felt like foolish self-indulgence. Most of what I bought I left in the packaging, in case I would need to take it back.

One Sunday in May, during the morning service, I was thinking about the names of our daughters, because the main theme of the service was grace. We had definitely experienced grace through the life of Jennifer Grace, but if Ruth were to die, would we still keep Joy as a middle name for her?

Just as that thought flew through my head, Gordon announced the next hymn, and as we sang verses three and four, they seemed to say a resounding 'yes':

> The joy of all who dwell above
> The joy of all below
> To whom He manifests His love
> And grants His name to know.
>
> To them, the cross, with all its shame
> With all its grace is given

Their name an everlasting name
Their joy the joy of heaven.[19]

Three weeks later, at another service, my thoughts were
bitter. It was another baptism, and I still couldn't be at one
without tears forming. I couldn't sing the words of the
blessing out loud and had to mouth them instead. 'We
didn't get to carry Jennifer into church,' I wrote in my
diary. 'A man in a dark suit carried her in for us in a tiny
white coffin.' Ruth kicked a lot throughout the service as
if to say, 'It's OK, Mum, I'm here.'

In October 1993, a very sad 'Personal View' entitled
'Trusting in our Carers' Judgement' had appeared in the
British Medical Journal (BMJ), describing very movingly the
heartache of a late termination of pregnancy because of
'foetal abnormality'. That baby too had been longed-for
and planned.

I was not in any way unsympathetic. Since Jennifer, I
could no longer be critical of anyone opting for
termination in those circumstances. Not that I thought that
TOP was the best choice, but because what we did was
hard and we needed all the assurances of God's love for
us and Jennifer that we got. Couples in our situation need
twenty-four hours a day, seven days a week support
throughout the remainder of the pregnancy and beyond,
in the way that we had known God's involvement to be
with us. We had also been greatly helped and encouraged
by friends, family, colleagues and our church – it would
have been so much more difficult on our own. The way we

---

[19] Thomas Kelly (1769–1855), 'The Head that Once was
Crowned with Thorns'.

had been cared for by Dr Matthew at the outset, being given those three days to adjust to the news of our baby's problems, was also critical. This couple's experience, on discovering that their child had abnormalities, was completely different, and had possibly influenced their choice. Termination had been 'strongly recommended' over a telephone call from the obstetrician following results from an amniocentesis which had taken place only one day after an abnormal scan. The author, the father of the unborn child, wrote:

> By this stage, looking back, I think that our capacity for logical thought had long since evaporated. I do not think that we were realistically able to make a truly voluntary and considered decision. It was as though we had been pushed on to a conveyor belt two weeks previously and were inexorably heading onwards impelled by a power beyond our control to a preordained destination.[20]

It felt that the alternative story needed to be told. I wrote and submitted my own article, using as a title words from John Bell's wonderful song, 'I Cannot Measure How You Heal'. And as had been John's experience in writing 'A Cradling Song', the words came strangely easily, as if God given. 'Peace and Pain' was published as a 'Personal View' in the *BMJ* in July 1994.

---

[20] Anthony McCluskey, 'Trusting in our Carers' Judgement', *British Medical Journal* (307) 30th October 1993, p1151. Used with permission.

On 3rd August 1994, when Jennifer would have been a year old, several things happened which seemed like careful timing on God's part, reminding us of His care. A letter popped through the letterbox from the General Secretary of the Christian Medical Fellowship (CMF) thanking me for the *BMJ* article. A beautiful basket of flowers, crammed full of every colour of fragrant freesia, arrived from my parents for 'Jennifer Grace's Day'. The phone rang, and it was Ann Norval, one of our elderly ladies from Ruchazie, to say that she and her husband, Davie, were thinking about us particularly 'as it must be about that time'.

Gordon and I marked the day by looking through the folder I had made, reminding ourselves of God's goodness and praying together, thanking God for Jennifer and for His care. Ruth kicked throughout!

Other surprising communications were to follow the *BMJ* article.

On 7th September, I was admitted to the Simpson Memorial Hospital for an induction of labour, as Ruth was overdue. Over the rest of that day, labour did not progress smoothly. Ruth became distressed, indicated by her heart rate dropping at times to as low as forty beats per minute, every time I had a contraction. What a relief when Dr Luke walked in and placidly suggested a further section, which would be performed by one of his team, Dr Laurie. Gordon, feeling totally helpless, was ushered to get scrubs on as I sat on a theatre trolley, an anaesthetist at my back injecting spinal anaesthetic, and a lovely, motherly theatre nurse at my front, telling me to hug her.

'Our first baby died,' I said, tearfully.

'I know,' she assured me. 'We're going to keep this one safe.'

And they did. Ruth Joy was lifted out, all red faced and gangly limbed. Gordon was able to watch her being weighed, then she was cocooned in a sheet and propped up at my right shoulder where, bright eyed, she seemed fascinated by the rest of the proceedings!

The following morning, Dr Laurie came in to my room for a chat. She asked if I was the Karen Palmer who had written the article 'Peace and Pain' in the *BMJ*. When I confirmed that I was, she told me what a privilege it was for her to have delivered Jennifer's little sister.

I found that physical recovery post-section was much quicker with a newborn to look after. And those few days after Ruth's birth were truly joyful times. On the morning I was to go home, however, I cried into my breakfast, because Jennifer ought to have been coming with her dad to pick her mum and her little sister up from hospital. I was so thankful for the discharge nurse, who talked with me about Jennifer, and for the friends who had mentioned her in their 'congratulations' cards.

Back at home, with Ruth safe and well, three letters arrived – one from the Labour Life Group, another from the journal *Healing and Wholeness* and the third from Pat Thomas who was compiling a book called *Every Birth is Different*[21] – all asking me if they could reproduce 'Peace

---

[21] Pat Thomas, *Every Birth is Different* (London: Headline Book Publishing, 1997). Pat Thomas, then editor of the *Association for Improvement in Maternity Services Journal* tells, in women's own

and Pain' in their publications. CMF wrote again, asking if I would write a longer article for their student magazine, *Nucleus*. Even the *Daily Record* contacted us, asking if they could interview and photograph us, and they produced a two-page spread.

The *Daily Record* article was an unexpected comfort to another mum. Our health visitor got in touch to say that one of her other patients would like to meet me. This lady had had a TOP following a scan diagnosis of anencephaly (a severe and fatal form of spina bifida). Appallingly, she had received a phone call when she got home from the scan giving her an appointment time the following day for the TOP. Now, many months later, her grief for her lost child was proving difficult to work through. Reading our very different experience in the *Daily Record* article helped her to see that she had been presented with TOP as a 'given', and had been rushed into it while she was still in shock, when it was not the only path she could have taken. She realised that she had not been given the gift of time we had in order to consider her decision, and that helped lessen her feelings of self-blame, allowing her to be kinder to herself.

In December 1994, we received a Christmas card from Dr Matthew. He told us that he had read 'Peace and Pain'

---

words, twenty-seven stories of childbirth. A text box which was inserted within my story recommended SATFA (Support Around Termination For Abnormality) for parents in our situation who might be considering TOP. I, personally, did not altogether agree with their approach. They later became known as ARC (Antenatal Results and Choices) which is mentioned in the useful links section at the back of this book.

and had been able to pass some copies on to others. God was using our experience with Jennifer in so many ways.

Meanwhile, Ruth, a happy and inquisitive baby, was keeping us busy. Her only unsettled time of day was when Gordon and I would have really liked to have been eating dinner but found ourselves, instead, taking turns to swing her in our arms in front of a video of *Mary Poppins*. I was very frustrated, however, with my impatience. I was impatient for her to grow, to move on, to achieve the next milestone, to fit the next set of clothes. It seemed crazy! One day, as I chided myself for the umpteenth time, I suddenly understood. The bigger Ruth got, the more solid and less vulnerable she got, the more independent she got, the less I would fear that she was someone who would linger with us only for a short while.

Good Housekeeping contacted us, asking if they could feature us in an article. The downside was that the photographer arrived on a wintery day but asked if he could take the photographs outside with us wearing summery clothes, as the article was for the June issue! They used the *BMJ* article in its entirety and asked me to write a postscript in order to mention Ruth.

I was still very sad when I thought about Jennifer, which was mostly on long pram walks with Ruth sound asleep. From time to time I would still cry about her. I missed talking about her most of all. Other people had long since stopped asking about her, and, of course, no one in our current church had known us when we were expecting her. Not that I wanted to talk about her all the time – I just longed to have her acknowledged.

Once again, there were ironies in terms of the people who did acknowledge her. Clare, who came to me for one-to-one church membership classes and had mild learning difficulties, as we discussed infant baptism began surmising how old Jennifer would be then, and how we would recognise each other in heaven. A lovely neighbour from Ruchazie who hadn't had an easy life phoned for a chat, and asked if Ruth looked like Jennifer.

At Mothers and Toddlers, Ruth crawled forwards for the first time and the other mums asked when she would be one. I wanted to say to someone, 'And Jennifer would have been two in August.' All the way up the road home, pushing the pram, Ruth sleeping, I felt sad. I thought about a good friend who had just moved to Edinburgh and whose son had been born a month before Jennifer. In July 1993, both very pregnant, we had met for a city centre walk, but I hadn't yet met her son and was anxious about it. What if I cried? That would be so unfair on my friend.

Once home, Ruth woke up but was tired and miserable, so I took her through to our bedroom so that she could see herself in the wall mirror – always guaranteed to cheer her up! Instead of looking at the mirror, however, she became totally fascinated by an embroidery[22] on the wall beside it,

---

[22] The embroidery was, 'I have inscribed your name on the palm of my hand', from Isaiah 49:16 (version unknown), which had been a great comfort to me during the pregnancy. We used it as the inscription on Jennifer's headstone but the full section reads, 'Can a woman forget her own baby and not love the child she bore? Even if a mother should forget her own child, I will never forget you. Jerusalem, I can never forget you!' (Isaiah 49:15-16). The words are addressed by God to

which Renee Johnstone, a close family friend, had made for us after Jennifer died. As Ruth turned from the embroidery to me, she gave me the most crinkly nosed smile. I felt so ministered to!

In grief, we never forget what we had, and we never forget what might have been. That year, the *BMJ* had also published a small 'Lesson from a Patient' by a general practitioner.[23] He told how an eighty-eight-year-old patient, whom he'd been seeing for more than twenty years, lingered at the end of her appointment one day. He waited, and after she had asked about the family photographs he kept on his desk, she quietly told him that many years previously she had had a baby girl who died. It would have been her little daughter's sixtieth birthday, and she had no one else to tell.

How wonderful it has been for us, over the years, when friends have acknowledged Jennifer in what they have written or said – in Christmas cards, at our other daughters' baptisms or on her birthday. My mother never failed to buy a beautiful card for us to remember 'Jennifer's Day', even in the last weeks of her life when she was able to neither write in it nor post it.

This is Jennifer Grace's Day and we join with you in missing her, yet thanking God for her life and the effect

---

Jerusalem, which symbolises His people as a whole. We have often taken them slightly out of context but they do, nonetheless, speak of God's character and His love.

[23] Oliver Samuel, 'An Outcome Indicator of Intimacy', *BMJ* (38) 4 June 1994.

of that life on us. We look forward to meeting her one day!
With love
Mum & Dad/Helen & Jim/Granny & Pa

When Ruth was two years old and five months, Sally Jane was born by elective Caesarean section. This time, Ruth had chosen the middle name, which was to be Michael if it was a boy, and Jane if a girl. *Mary Poppins* aficionados will appreciate the connection!

If anything, I had been more anxious during Sally's pregnancy. I was much less aware of movement – possibly contributed to by the fact that Sally's knees and elbows weren't as pointy as Ruth's! I also felt greedy! Gordon and I had always planned to have two children, and here we were, having a third. Shouldn't I just be content with our one healthy child? This time I found support through SANDS, who had a 'next-pregnancy support group' in Edinburgh.

After she was born, Sally's facial resemblance to Jennifer was both wonderful to me and unsettling. She had a few small, immaterial imperfections including mild tongue tie and a three-dimensional pink birthmark called a strawberry naevus, which made me wonder if there might be something more sinister underlying it all.

Looking back, I wonder if I might have been suffering from mild postnatal depression during Sally's first six months. Gordon turned forty in the July and the effort of trying to think of how to make it a celebration was totally beyond me. Sally survived it all, full of character, creativity and rascally mischief – our unexpected bonus child.

At some point after our move to Edinburgh, the daughter of an elderly lady in our church, having heard about Jennifer, got in touch. Seven years previously, her son had been born with Patau's syndrome[24] and had died shortly after birth.[25] She told us of a support organisation called SOFT (Support Organisation for Trisomy 13/18 and related disorders) which she felt might be of help to us, even though Jennifer had not had such a disorder. SOFT was happy to take us on board, and support came by way of a regular magazine with contributions by SOFT families – some who had chosen TOP; some who, like us, had continued the pregnancies; some whose children had been stillborn or died shortly after birth; some whose children lived for months and even years. Reading other people's stories was indeed helpful and I continued to subscribe to the magazine for some time.

SOFT was beginning to produce booklets which could be given to hospital staff and to parents following diagnosis. They invited members to share their memories and experiences. In July 1998, its first edition of the booklet *Your Unborn Baby – Facts for Families*[26] was published, including large sections of the article I had written for CMF's *Nucleus* magazine.

---

[24] A chromosomal disorder also known as Trisomy 13.
[25] Esther Shreeve tells her own story in *The Gingerbread House: A Journey of Faith Through Bereavement* (Peterborough: Inspire, 2005).
[26] Your Unborn Baby – Facts for Families (SOFT UK 1998).

In 2006, Sally was nine years old and Ruth twelve, and we were living in East Kilbride. Gordon was the minister of Claremont Parish Church and I was a part-time specialty psychiatrist in a mental health resource centre in Glasgow. The girls had known about Jennifer for many years, happily accepting her as part of our family, and Ruth would sometimes correct people if they referred to her as the oldest sister.

A slightly alarming request came, via CMF, asking if I would tell Jennifer's story at an event at the House of Commons. Organised by the 'Alive and Kicking' campaign, this was to be the launch of *Defiant Birth*, written by Australian activist Melinda Tankard Reist.[27] Gordon's and my choices had not felt 'defiant' at the time, but reading Melinda's book gave an insight into the opposition that many parents in similar situations had encountered.

At that time, Gordon Brown was Chancellor of the Exchequer. In January 2002, he and his wife, Sarah, had lost their first child, also named Jennifer, at just ten days old. Given that he was a fellow Scot and that his father had been a church minister, I expected Mr Brown might welcome a copy of CH4 with the relevance of hymn 733 to his situation, and the serendipity of its tune being called 'Jennifer'. I therefore took a copy of CH4 with me, wrote a note in it while sitting on the south bank of the Thames, and asked one of the MPs at the event to kindly pass it on to him. I still have the warm and gracious letter of thanks

27 Melinda Tankard Reist, *Defiant Birth: Women Who Resist Medical Eugenics* (Spinifex Press, Melbourne: 2006).

Gordon Brown wrote to me in characteristic black felt pen, while he was on holiday:

The words of the hymn to Jennifer are very moving indeed and reflect exactly the feelings we have experienced too.
Gordon Brown, August 2006[28]

---

[28] Personal correspondence. Used with kind permission. Gordon and Sarah Brown set up the Jennifer Brown Research laboratory in memory of their daughter Jennifer – 'set up to improve the lives of women who suffer complications in pregnancy and the newborn period'.

A Promise Fulfilled

The words 'everywhere she had been, there grew flowers', given to me after Jennifer's death in hospital, gave me purpose at the time and also, in some remarkable way, turned out to have been a promise.

In July 2014, just two weeks before what would have been Jennifer's twenty-first birthday, we found ourselves not in Rottenrow Hospital itself, for it had been demolished, but in the beautiful Rottenrow Gardens which had been created on its site.

The occasion was an opening event for the Commonwealth Games – Stephen Beazley's 'the Perch Festival' – and Sally, dressed as a crow, was playing her flute with the National Youth Orchestra's senior orchestra. More than 200 performers, in what was described as a 'magnificent menagerie', should have completely held my attention. Instead, what captivated me (apart from Sally, obviously) were the beautiful banks of fragrant lavender. Everywhere Jennifer had been, there grew flowers!

Glory to God

Because we never knew the cause of Jennifer's problems, there was always a niggle in my mind that something I had done in the early days of pregnancy might have been to blame. Those fears seemed justified when potential dangers of dentistry work using mercury came to light and were reported on the national news. I had had emergency dental work involving a mercury filling when only around five weeks pregnant with Jennifer. That thought continued to torment me from time to time – after all, the need for the filling was most likely a result of my very undisciplined chocolate consumption!

How wonderful, then, years later in Claremont church, to be introduced to the song 'Rejoice, Rejoice, Christ is in You' by Graham Kendrick, which includes these verses:

> God is at work in us, His purpose to perform
> Building a kingdom of power not of words
> Where things impossible, by faith shall be made possible
> Let's give the glory to Him now.
>
> Though we are weak His grace is everything we need
> We're made of clay but His treasure is within

He turns our weaknesses into His opportunities
So that the glory goes to Him.[29]

Whatever the cause of Jennifer's problems, even if in some way it was due to some weakness of mine, our gracious God had turned it into so many opportunities to help others, and to speak to others of His love and care. I could finally let go of those feelings of failure and guilt.

Ruth and Sally had to work through their own thoughts and feelings about Jennifer, learning about a big sister they had never known but who had made such an impact on their parents' lives. Sally was able to express some of her questions in an essay for school when she was fifteen:

> I wanted to thrust her fragile structure above mine with pride and yell, 'This is my sister, beautifully designed!'
> But I didn't.
> For this masterpiece was unfinished. Monet had left his painting unsigned. She was abstract art, modern art. A raw, misunderstood beauty. My sister, a smudge on the great family tree. A mistake, coloured over the lines. A scribble to be rubbed out. It was like God had had artist's block. Did he forget to finish her, or purposefully leave her incomplete?

[29] Verses 2 and 3 of Graham Kendrick's 'Rejoice, Rejoice, Christ is in You', Thankyou Music, Capitol CMG Publishing, Integrity Music. Used with permission.

'Why does God allow suffering?' was a question Gordon and I never asked. The world is a fallen place. The fullness of its redemption, already won by Christ, is yet to come. Suffering, for the Christian, however, is ameliorated. God breathes into it His grace. As the psalmist says, 'the LORD is your shade at your right hand' (Psalm 121:5b, NIV). He cushions us. Jennifer certainly seemed to experience that in a very real way, and bore none of the wounds that such a profound lack of amniotic fluid can cause. Gordon and I were cushioned too – our gracious God helped us see Jennifer as a child who was precious and loved by Him; He gave us hospital staff, family, colleagues, friends and church folk who supported us wonderfully. Care and prayers both carried us and cooried[30] us. We weren't alone in our hurting – our pain and distress were shared by those who cared for us. And as they shared our suffering, yet saw how God helped us and sustained us, they in turn were blessed. Many spoke of the impact Jennifer's life had had on them. The comfort God gave us was salve not just for us, but also for others.

The sorrow we felt was mixed with joy: the joy of knowing God with us and answering our prayers. As all who have lost a loved one know, the grief is ongoing, but so are God's promises! Bereavement is not a moment in time but something you carry with you for life – calculating what age they would be, seeing their absence at every family event, knowing that your family is, in that sense, forever incomplete. But Gordon and I could trust God's promises and know that Jennifer was totally safe

---

[30] Scottish word which, in this context, means 'cosily cuddled' or 'lovingly swaddled'.

with Him. All that we had been through brought richness – in relationships with God and others, and in all sorts of other, different ways.

I still miss Jennifer and long for her, but I do feel really privileged to have carried her and to be her mum. Through her, God taught us and brought us so much. We are rich indeed to have had her, and through her have had such a clear demonstration of God's love and care for the damaged and vulnerable, and of God's intimate involvement with each of us. My memories of her are lasting treasure.

And so, as for many, our suffering has been life-changing and transforming. Despite having been a Christian for more than twenty years by the time I was carrying Jennifer, it is my experience with her and all God did then that I most look back to for strength – a bit like the Israelites remembering their escape from Egypt! That experience made all I knew in my head as theory become three-dimensional. Having grown up in a Christian home, I didn't have a dramatic conversion story. Now Jennifer is a large part of my testimony. I had never before known God speak so loudly. All that He prepared for us that Easter week to help us still blows my mind.

I'm different since Jennifer. She, and all God did through her, are forever part of me. At work, I discovered greater empathy for the parents of my patients – a greater understanding of all the varieties of loss experienced when a loved one develops a life-changing illness. My expectation of God working in my life and in the lives of others increased.

How does faith grow? It grows by trusting God to keep His promises and finding that He always does.

Ruth and Sally are a great joy to us and have enriched our lives in many ways. Gordon and I are so thankful for both of them, and as each of us is formed by the experiences we have, so Jennifer, though she died before they were born, has been part of their formation as people. More than words can express is our delight that Jennifer's story helps them know that, no matter what, they too are our treasure and they too are precious to God.

We always talked about Jennifer as a member of our family, just one that Sally and I had never met, so I have always understood that she is as important to and as loved by my parents as we are. I think this is how I first understood the concept of unconditional love; Jennifer didn't earn my parents' love by being good or clever or interesting. They love her because she is their daughter. As a result of how we talked about her, I have always felt secure in my parents' – and my heavenly Father's – love for me.
Ruth

I was always proud to speak of Jennifer at school. I would correct people who labelled me as 'one of two sisters' – I was one of three and wanted them to know that.

And I think this was the reason: I wanted everyone to know how my parents loved. That they held what others would call 'broken' or a 'mistake' and called her beautiful and grace. They loved her because she was theirs.

I'm proud of my parents' words on these pages because it tells the story of them lovingly sacrificing for the precious child they called 'daughter'. And all the way through this story are threads of a greater story, of a greater love and of a greater sacrifice.

Sally

After Jennifer's death, our dear friend Janet Robertson said that when Jennifer arrived in heaven, there would be great rejoicing and celebration because of all she achieved in her short life. But the greatest praise is to our wonderful God who is right here with His people, always keeps His promises and can be totally trusted. All the glory belongs to Him.

Appendix: 'A Cradling Song'

1. We cannot care for you the way we wanted,
    or cradle you, or listen for your cry;
    but, separated as we are by silence,
    love will not die.

2. We cannot watch you growing into childhood,
    nor find a new uniqueness every day;
    but special as you would have been among us
    you still will stay.

3. We cannot know the pain or the potential
    which passing years would summon or reveal;
    but for that true fulfilment Jesus promised
    we hope and feel.

4. So through the mess of anger, grief, and tiredness,
    through tensions which are not yet reconciled,
    we give to God the worship of our sorrow
    and our dear child.

5. Lord, in your arms, which cradle all creation,
    we rest and place our baby beyond death,
    believing that she now, alive in heaven,
    breathes with your breath.

This hymn may be read aloud while the following sequence is played.

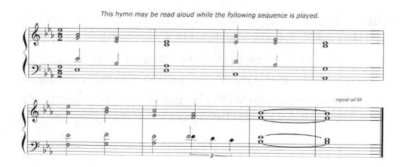

JENNIFER

This arrangement copyright © Sally Palmer 2020

141

Acknowledgements

As you've read this book, it will have been clear that we didn't travel the journey on our own. There was a whole army on our side – caring, praying, phoning, cooking (principally Janet Robertson and our mothers), writing cards and letters, listening, keeping me company. I am so sorry that I'm not able to mention everybody by name, but we are so grateful for each one. Ruchazie church family was a conduit of God's grace, our safe place, and we were wonderfully held by them. So too my parents by the Stirling Baptist church family who showered us with cards and letters assuring us of their prayers. The Church of Scotland's presbytery clerk for Glasgow, Alex Cunningham, wrote kindly to Gordon offering any help required. 'Dr Matthew', his team at Rottenrow and my midwife looked after us beautifully.

Colleagues and friends were wonderful. John Baird and my fellow psychiatric trainees at the time – Kim Hickey, Frances Burnett, Jacqui Anderson and Debbie Mason – were conscientious and attentive in the way they looked after me. Along with Suzanne Catterall, then administrator at the Douglas Inch Centre and other colleagues from the State Hospital, they all came to the funeral. I'm so grateful for everyone who came and stood by us on such a hard day. Our wonderful GP, Dr Spence, was there too. I remember him laughing at my mother, who in her typical way was trying to organise everyone. We really dumped some friends in it, so thank you to Gordon's amazing university friends for their part in the funeral service – Alistair Drummond who conducted it and read the tribute, Jim Reid who read the Wolterstorff chapter and John Payne who played the piano so beautifully. And thank you too to Andy Pyott for the tough task of fielding that early phone call from me when we needed advice about CVS. And talking of phone calls, Andrzej Prach phoned faithfully every month of the pregnancy just to see how we were doing. Jack Kellet, with whom Gordon did his probationary period, has never failed to mention Jennifer in the annual Christmas card he sends us.

The greatest delight in writing this book was that the need to seek permissions from anyone mentioned resulted in renewed contacts after many years. And so, because some of them plan to read it, I can record my very grateful thanks here to Derek, Darren, Jimmy, Elaine, Karen and Bryan. I'm hoping we can meet up soon for hot chocolate!

Many who cared for us are no longer with us – our parents, Janet Robertson, Janet Anderson and many precious elderly and not so elderly folk who were part of Ruchazie church. Safe with Jesus.

We owe a huge debt to the Wild Goose Resource Group for the great resource of their beautifully crafted liturgies, prayers and songs, particularly John L Bell for 'A Cradling Song' and the late Graham Maule. God bless you, John, who have blessed so many others.

Thank you to all who gave permission to include their words in this book – also Gordon Brown, the *British Medical Journal*, Christian Medical Fellowship, Capitol CTG and Wm Eerdmans.

John Bell is among the long list of kind friends and associates who have kindly taken the trouble to read the manuscript and provide commendations – David Bebbington, Doug Gay, Margaret Masson, Stephen Chester, Colin Sinclair, Judith Keefe and Peter Saunders. Thank you all.

Rosemary Luke, Susan Finlay and Gordon have gone one step further – not only reading the book more than once but very helpfully making suggestions for improving it. I'm really humbled by the time you've spent on my account and very grateful.

Instant Apostle do wonderful wrap-around care for authors and have guided me gently through this whole process. Nicki Copeland might be the most patient person I have ever come across. Thank you too to Sheila Jacobs for her thorough work as reader and copy editor, to Anne Rogers for all her work on the cover and to Kathryn Weller, Amanda Pilz and Nigel Freeman.

Robin Love (Ruth's father-in-law), with his clever photographic skills, and knitter extraordinaire Kimberley from Heidihousecrafts helped provide a perfect East End of Glasgow photograph for the book cover, at Hogganfield Loch. You are both stars. Thank you!

Finally, the greatest thanks must go to those to whom I also owe the greatest apology. Sally, to whom I emailed the manuscript, thereby leaving her to read through it in tears, hundreds of miles away from home. Ruth and her husband, Stuart, who suffered the very terrible timing of a mother/mother-in-law finishing off a manuscript about the death of her first child as they waited for theirs. Anna Corrie Love's safe arrival has brought great joy and thanksgiving.

Gordon had high hopes that with my retirement would come a much tidier house, but so far, no change. He's read the book over and over, and with his characteristic indulgence of me has put up with it being yet one more of my obsessions. I am beyond grateful to be his wife and to have shared the joys and sadnesses of parenthood with such a man.

And to our God, the perfect Father whose love lasts for ever, the Son who offers forgiveness for all our failings and the Spirit who lives in and with His people, all thanks and praise to You.

Useful Links and Resources[31]

Under the Rainbow is an online Christian resource for those affected by baby loss, infertility, adoption and fostering and contains practical information, reading recommendations and testimonials.
www.undertherainbow.org.uk

Hope Deferred runs conferences for those experiencing baby loss and infertility, as well as anyone, including ministers and pastors, who want to better understand how to support parents in such situations. The conferences are run by a team of Christians who have personal and professional experience in these areas.
www.hopedeferred.co.uk

SOFT (Support Organisation for Trisomy 13/18 and related disorders) primarily provides support for families affected by Trisomy 13 (Patau's syndrome) and Trisomy 18 (Edwards' syndrome). Jennifer had no diagnosed syndrome but SOFT was still happy to let me join. Members include those who have had terminations of

---

[31] Not every organisation listed below shares the values expressed in this book. Please have a look at them yourself before recommending them to anyone else.

pregnancy as well as those whose children live for months or many years. Support is via trained volunteers who all have experience of receiving a diagnosis of Trisomy 13, 18 or a related condition, and there is also a SOFT families Facebook group.
www.soft.org.uk

Care for the Family is a national charity with a Christian foundation aiming to help those who face difficulties in family life, including raising children with additional needs. Its website includes podcasts and testimonials, and it organises holidays for single-parent families as well as day conferences for bereaved parents.
www.careforthefamily.org.uk

ARC (Antenatal Results and Choices) offers parents non-directive information and support during and after antenatal screening, for as long as they need it, whether they decide to continue with the pregnancy or not. Formerly known as Support Around Termination For Abnormality (SATFA), the name change was to reflect an expansion in its aims. It has a UK helpline, 0845 077 2290 or 0207 713 7486 from a mobile – lines open Monday to Friday 10am-5.30pm.
www.arc-uk.org

The Compassionate Friends offers support for family members after the death of a child, whatever the circumstances. Support takes the form of an online forum, Facebook group, local support groups and a telephone

helpline 0345 123 2304 available every day of the year from 10am-4pm and 7pm-10pm.
www.tcf.org.uk

Together for Short Lives supports families with information, networking and access to care, when a child's life is expected to be short. Its *Perinatal Pathway for Babies with Palliative Care Needs* gives guidance to professionals in order to help them introduce elements of palliative care in the antenatal period when a life-threatening condition is identified in early pregnancy. As part of this, it encourages relationship-building between local NHS obstetric services, children's hospices and palliative care charities. It has a Facebook group and its website contains factsheets and guides. Its helpline is 0808 8088 100 (10am-4pm Monday to Friday, closed at weekends and on bank holidays).
www.togetherforshortlives.org.uk

Children's Hospices can work alongside antenatal care in the NHS to provide perinatal palliative care. In Scotland, the **Children's Hospice Association Scotland (CHAS)** accepts self-referrals as well as referrals from General Practitioners and antenatal departments. Care lines: 01577 865777 (Rachel House KY13 8FX) or 01389 722055 (Robin House G83 8LX).
www.chas.org.uk

SANDS (Stillbirth and Neonatal Death Society) offers support to anyone affected by a baby who is stillborn or who dies shortly after birth. It runs local groups, an online forum, a UK-wide befriender network, annual memorial events, and has a bereavement support app for parents, families, carers and health professionals. Its helpline is 0808 164 3332 or helpline@sands.org.uk, and the team are available to respond from 9.30am to 5.30pm Monday to Friday, and in addition 5.30pm to 9.30pm on Tuesdays and Thursdays.

www.sands.org.uk

Bibliography

A Gift of Time: Continuing Your Pregnancy When Your Baby's Life is Expected to be Brief, Amy Kuebelbeck and Deborah L Davis (Baltimore, MD: John Hopkins University Press, 2011).

A handbook for parents and professionals alike, this is a wonderful resource and companion. Contents are listed in great detail over three pages in order to allow you to dip in, rather than read it straight through (which would, emotionally, be very hard going). Compiled from dozens of questionnaires and interviews, it shares the experiences of parents who have already travelled that journey – journeys of grief, but also of joy, as they adjusted to a very different pregnancy from what they had expected.

Defiant Birth: Women Who Resist Medical Eugenics, Melinda Tankard Reist (Melbourne: Spinifex Press, 2006).

Using nineteen stories of women (including that of Amy Kuebelbeck – see above) who continued pregnancies despite pressure to do otherwise, this is an alarming look at the subtle politics at work in our societies.

When the Dream is Shattered: Coping With Child-bearing Difficulties, Judith and Michael Murray (Adelaide: Lutheran Publishing House, 1988).

Sadly now out of print and never updated, this was my guidebook.

Startling Beauty, Heather Gemmen (Eastbourne: Kingsway Publications, 2004).

The remarkable and honest account of a woman who was raped in her own home and, after the initial instinct of wanting to end the pregnancy, continued with it. Heather's writing is exquisite and she paints a wonderful picture of her local church and a God who loves us despite all our flaws and failures.

The Shaming of the Strong: The Challenge of an Unborn Life, Sarah Williams (Eastbourne: Kingsway Publications, 2005).

The story of Cerian, Sarah's third daughter, is beautifully told and can be read in a few hours. Living in a high-powered world of academic theologians, Sarah reflects on human worth and God's love for the weak and damaged. Her experiences with professionals would make it a helpful book for any caregiver, and it contains helpful insights about ways in which other family members can be helped.

The Gingerbread House: A Journey of Faith Through Bereavement, Esther Shreeve (Peterborough: Inspire, 2005).

Currently out of print but available second-hand, this is the story of Ben who, without any indication of problems during the pregnancy, was born with Trisomy 13 (Patau's syndrome) and died shortly after birth. Esther interweaves her thoughts and reflections throughout, making this a piercingly honest and helpful account of a family coming to terms with child loss. It contains the wonderful poems of Jessica Aidley which, as far as I am aware, do not appear anywhere else in print.

Lament for a Son, Nicholas Wolterstorff (Grand Rapids, MI: William B Eerdmans Publishing Co, 1987).

This was out of print for a while, but thankfully no longer. Gordon and I have certainly purchased and given away many copies over the years. The journal of a father whose son dies, aged twenty-five, entries range in length from a few lines to just over three pages. It's a small book, but packed with profundity. Laying himself bare, Wolterstorff reveals an anatomy of grief – hurts, regrets, sudden thoughts, flashes of insight and a gradual working through. Essential reading for the bereaved and caregiver alike, who wonder where God is in it all.

When Grief is Raw: Songs for Times of Sorrow and Bereavement, John L Bell and Graham Maule (Glasgow: Wild Goose Resource Group, Wild Goose Publications, the Iona Community, 1997).

It feels especially poignant to be typing this a few short weeks after the sad and premature death of Graham, one of the co-authors. A collection of songs, many inspired by the psalms and other scriptures, they are mostly intended for congregational singing at memorial or funeral services but can also be used as solos or readings.

A Wee Worship Book: Fourth Incarnation (Glasgow: Wild Goose Worship Group, Wild Goose Publications, 2004).

This is a fully revised and expanded version of the original book, our copy now totally dog-eared, which we used so frequently in Ruchazie Parish Church and which has remained a regular companion of Gordon's during thirty-three years of ministry. Containing morning, daytime and evening liturgies as well as liturgies for Communion and other special services, there are prayers, songs and responsive readings. Not just a short cut for hard-pressed ministers, it's also a treasure trove of inspired and beautifully crafted phrases, touching real life in all its joy and sorrow and encouraging meaningful and honest worship.